Happily Ever After

Other books in the Wisdom & Warnings® series

From Divorce Mess to Happiness

Tips From the Quad

Let Them Fly

The Badass Woman

Because You Care

Our library of wisdom keeps growing!
Check out the full list anytime at wisdomandwarnings.com
or simply scan the QR code.

Happily Ever After

*Daily Wisdom for a Marriage
that Lasts*

Jen Fort
From the Wisdom & Warnings® Series

Disclaimer

The author of **Happily Ever After** is not a licensed therapist. Because of this, this book is presented solely for educational and entertainment purposes and is not intended to replace the advice of a physician, professional coach, therapist, or other qualified professionals.

This book was created with the assistance of various resources, including AI as a brainstorming tool to help organize ideas and enhance clarity. However, all insights, concepts, and creative content are entirely the author's.

Cover design by Margaret Cogswell

Edited by Mark Nyman

This collection of Wisdom & Warnings is dedicated to every couple creating their "happily ever after."

And to Tara, who tossed tradition like confetti and proved that happily ever after is even better with bridesmen by your side. May your story keep unfolding with laughter and love.

What People Are Saying

"Day 230 has been my favorite. Your passion really comes through and this advice is necessary, especially in an age where divorce is so prevalent."

- *Mark N.*

Share Your Wisdom!

Wisdom & Warnings consists of nearly 8,000 carefully curated nuggets of wisdom across dozens of topics for life's milestones, ranging from relationships to parents/children to education and career, plus fun topics for living your best life.

Engage with the Wisdom & Warnings community for ongoing encouragement through life's milestones.

www.wisdomandwarnings.com

Facebook: www.facebook.com/wisdomandwarnings/

Instagram: @wisdomandwarnings

Email: hello@wisdomandwarnings.com

Contents

My Story

There's something magical about hearing the right words at just the right time—a spark of wisdom that can brighten a day, guide a decision, or even change the course of a life. I've always been drawn to those small but powerful truths. From an early age, I found myself captivated by people's stories—their struggles, triumphs, and the nuggets of wisdom they carried. Every person I met seemed to have something unique to teach me, and I couldn't help but ask: *What's your lesson?*

That curiosity became the seed of a passion I call *Wisdom & Warnings*—a lifelong quest to learn from the experiences of others. Over the years, I turned conversations into a collection of insights. Friends, family, and even strangers at the grocery store shared their advice with me, often without realizing how profound their words were. By the time I looked back, I had gathered over 8,000 pieces of advice—a treasure chest of wisdom just waiting to be shared. But for the longest time, I didn't.

Self-doubt became my shadow. *What if I fail? What if no one cares?* Those questions kept me in a cycle of "someday" and "not yet." I tinkered with the idea for over a decade, hesitating to commit fully. Deep down, though, I couldn't shake the feeling that this treasure wasn't meant to stay hidden. Whenever I thought about shelving the project, a little voice whispered, "Life is too short not to learn from each other." It felt selfish not to share, but fear has a way of making even the brightest ideas feel impossible. That, my friends, is a topic for another time.

Then, life gave me an unexpected push. I lost my job—a moment that felt devastating at first but turned out to be the break I needed. Suddenly, I had time to reflect, and one thing became crystal clear: it was now or never. Those whispers urging me to share my collection became impossible to ignore. I realized that I didn't need to be perfect or polished; I just needed to start.

So, I took a leap of faith with no formal writing experience and zero understanding of the publishing world. That leap became the *365 Days of Wisdom & Warnings* book series. Along the way, I've made mistakes, learned lessons, and celebrated every small victory. More than anything, I've realized that when you listen to the quiet whispers of your heart, you're led to something greater than fear: purpose.

If this journey has taught me anything, it's that the world needs what only you can offer. You might feel unqualified or unsure, but someone out there is waiting for what you have to give. My wish for you is this: trust those quiet whispers, silence the doubts—whether they're yours or someone else's—and chase what sets your soul on fire. Your passion could be the light that sparks someone else's journey. And isn't that the real magic?

I'll be cheering you on,

Jen

Introduction

Happily ever after isn't something you're handed—it's something you build, choice by choice, day by day. Your wedding may be the spark, but the real story begins afterward, when the flowers have wilted and it's just the two of you learning how to live, love, and grow together. Marriage is equal parts joy and effort. It's not about perfection, but about presence, forgiveness, and the small daily gestures that remind your partner, "I still choose you."

The wisdom in these pages comes from real people—some who've walked side by side for decades, and others who didn't make it but were willing to share what they wish they had done differently. Both perspectives matter. Sometimes the best lessons come from hindsight, from the missed chances to listen more, fight less, or cherish what really mattered.

Inside, you'll find 365 nuggets of encouragement, humor, and hard-earned truth. Use them as daily reminders, discussion starters, or gentle nudges back toward connection. Because happily ever after isn't guaranteed—it's created, protected, and renewed every single day

.

Chapter 1

You Said Yes, Now What?
A strong marriage starts long before the vows

Day 1

Each relationship milestone is the start of something new.

Your engagement is a beginning. So is your wedding day. Your first fight, your first home, your first anniversary, each one marks the start of a new chapter. Marriage isn't about "settling down," it's about stepping up. It's about building something that didn't exist before, such as a shared life, filled with intention, laughter, and love that deepens with time. Each milestone gives you a fresh chance to recommit, to dream bigger, and to lean on each other in new ways. You're not just celebrating moments, you're creating momentum.

Don't be surprised if it feels like you're starting over again and again. A strong marriage doesn't stay the same; it evolves. It stretches, shifts, and surprises you. What matters most is showing up repeatedly with open hands, an open heart, and the willingness to build something extraordinary out of the everyday. This is your beginning, and there are so many more to come.

 Ask each other: What makes now the right time to get married?

Day 2

A good marriage is often 75% luck, 20% trust, and 5% lust.

A good marriage isn't all planning and perfection; it's part serendipity. About 75% of it is luck: meeting the right person at the right time, with the right kind of crazy that matches your own. Then comes 20% trust—that deep, steady knowing that you've got each other's backs, even when things get messy. And finally, there's that last 5% of lust and passion. The spark that keeps things playful, flirty, and fun over the years. It doesn't have to be constant, just present. Marriage isn't a perfect formula, but when these parts come together, it creates something of lasting beauty.

Day 3

Learn early how to cope effectively with crisis.

Every relationship will face a crisis at some point. You simply can't avoid it. What matters most is *how* you handle a crisis. Everyone does it differently, but coping productively means focusing on the problem, not turning on each other. Take a breath, listen with the goal of understanding, and speak respectfully, even when it's hard. Crisis can feel overwhelming, but it's also an opportunity to build trust and deepen your connection. You don't have to have all the answers, just a shared commitment to face it together. Growth often comes through the mess, not around it. When you handle it well, you come out stronger together.

 Something to talk about: Is the way we handle conflict healthy?

Day 4

Don't keep financial secrets.

Financial secrets can quietly erode the foundation of a rock-solid relationship. Whether it's hidden debt, secret spending, or a "just in case" stash, it sends the message that trust has limits and that can hurt more than any dollar amount. Being open about money doesn't mean you have to merge every cent, but it *does* mean being honest about your habits, goals, and concerns. Talk about what money means to each of you, whether that means security, freedom or stress, because it's rarely just about numbers. Transparency builds trust, and trust is the real currency of a lasting relationship.

Day 5

Don't lose your individuality once you become engaged.

Getting engaged is exciting; it's the start of a shared future, but it shouldn't mean the end of your individuality. The healthiest relationships are made by two whole people who choose to grow *together*, not merge into one identity (even though some wedding vows talk about *two becoming one*). Keep nurturing your own personal passions, friendships, and goals, even as you plan your life as a couple. Your uniqueness is part of what your partner fell in love with in the first place! Staying true to yourself makes the relationship stronger, not weaker. Build a life *together* while you remember to keep being *you*.

 Ask each other: What does money mean to you? Security, freedom, stress, or something else?

Day 6

The smallest gestures mean the most.

Over time, it's rarely the grand vacations or fancy gifts that stand out; it's the quiet moments, the small gestures, and the simple acts of love that leave the deepest mark. The cup of coffee brought without asking, the text that says, "thinking of you," and the hand squeeze during a hard moment are the things we carry with us. Life gets busy, and relationships evolve, but taking the time to show up in small, thoughtful ways builds a lasting foundation. One day, you'll look back and realize it wasn't the big stuff that made your love story; it was the little things done often.

Day 7

Find an APP or game that helps you learn about each other.

One of the simplest ways to deepen your bond is to turn connection into a game. Find an app or game that helps you learn about each other, because who said personal growth can't be fun? Try apps like *Paired*, which offers daily relationship questions, or *Gottman Card Decks* for research-backed conversation starters. You can also grab a scratch-off adventure book like *The Adventure Challenge: Couples Edition* for spontaneous date ideas. Whether you're laughing over silly prompts or discovering something new about your partner's dreams, these tools spark connection and create fun memories before the stress of the wedding kicks in.

 Conversation starter: If we want kids, how many? Why this number?

Day 8

A solid relationship has your back when life gets messy.

When life throws its curveballs, having a solid relationship is like having emotional armor. It doesn't stop the challenges from coming, but it gives you a safe place to land when they do. Knowing someone truly has your back makes the weight of the world feel a little lighter. You don't have to face every struggle alone; instead, you have a partner to lean on, laugh with, and navigate the mess beside you. Love doesn't erase the hard stuff, but it makes you more resilient. In a world full of uncertainty, connection is your strongest defense.

Day 9

Appreciation is always appreciated. Expectations often lead to disappointment.

Appreciation is one of those small habits with a significant impact. A simple "thank you" or "I see what you did there" can go a long way in making your partner feel valued. On the other hand, unspoken expectations can be sneaky; they build silently and often end in frustration when the other person has no idea what you were hoping for. Clear communication beats silent hoping every time. Choose to notice the effort, not just the outcome. When appreciation flows more freely than expectation, your relationship feels lighter, more joyful, and a lot less like a guessing game.

 Ask each other: What are you most excited about during our marriage?

Day 10

Be their calm in the chaos.

It's easy to feel like just another face in the crowd, especially when life gets noisy. But to someone, such as your partner, a close friend, or a child, you are *everything*. You're the steady presence, the safe place, the one who matters most. That kind of connection is powerful, and it reminds us that our impact isn't measured by how many people know our name, but by how deeply we're known by one. Don't underestimate your role in someone's life. You might be their calm in the chaos, their home base, and their whole world wrapped up in one person.

Day 11

A strong marriage depends on a foundation of friendship.

Passion might light the spark, but it's friendship that keeps the fire going when life gets real. A lasting marriage is built on shared laughter, inside jokes, mutual respect, and the ease of being fully yourself with someone who sees you. Friendship in marriage means showing up for the big wins and the messy middles. It's cheering each other on, listening when it matters most, and still genuinely liking one another after the honeymoon glow fades. Don't just be lovers, be teammates, co-conspirators, partners in crime, and best friends.

 Something to talk about: If you could change one thing about your childhood, what would it be? Why?

Day 12

Make peace with your past for a better tomorrow.

The past has a sneaky way of showing up uninvited, especially in relationships. Old wounds, past mistakes, or unresolved issues can subtly influence how you perceive your partner or respond in tense moments. That's why making peace with your past is so important. It doesn't mean pretending it didn't happen or forgetting the pain; it means understanding it, learning from it, and choosing not to let it take the driver's seat. When you've done the work to heal, you're free to show up in the present with clarity, kindness, and trust. Let the past be a teacher, not a traitor.

Day 13

"Before you marry, keep your eyes wide open. Once you're married, keep them half shut." — Benjamin Franklin

Before marriage, it's smart to be all eyes and ears so you can notice the habits, values, and red flags that might affect your future together. This is the time for honest conversations and clear-eyed decisions. But once you've said, "I do," it's just as wise to practice a little selective vision. This doesn't mean ignoring big issues; it means choosing to let the small stuff slide. Those little quirks that once seemed charming might later test your patience, but grace goes a long way. A happy marriage isn't about perfection; it's about knowing when to speak up and when to simply smile and carry on.

 Conversation starter: If we want kids, how do you feel about one parent not working to raise them?

Day 14

Loving someone gives you courage; being loved by someone gives you strength.

There's something incredibly grounding about being deeply loved; it's like having an emotional anchor in a world that's constantly shifting. That kind of love gives you strength because you know someone truly sees you and still chooses you, flaws and all. But loving someone deeply? That's where the courage comes in. It means showing up, being vulnerable, and risking your heart, even when there are no guarantees. Real love calls you to be brave, to grow, and to open your heart again and again. When both strength and courage show up, that's where real connection thrives.

Day 15

Compliment each other often.

Compliments are like little love notes for the soul, and in a relationship, they never go out of style. Whether it's "you look great today" or "thanks for always making me laugh," small words of affirmation go a long way in keeping the connection strong. Life gets busy, and it's easy to assume the other person *knows* how you feel, but don't let kindness stay stuck in your head. Say it out loud. Regular compliments build confidence, boost mood, and remind your partner that they're seen and appreciated. And let's be honest, who doesn't like a little love-fueled ego boost?

 Ask each other: What compliment have you received that made you feel like a million bucks?

Day 16

Read Love and Respect by Dr. Emerson Eggerichs

Love and Respect by Dr. Emerson Eggerichs is a relationship game-changer for many couples. The core idea is simple: in general, women desire love, and men want respect, and when either is missing, it creates what Eggerichs calls the "Crazy Cycle." The book explores how minor miscommunications can spiral out of control unless we intentionally meet each other's core emotional needs. It's full of real-life examples, practical advice, and gentle challenges to help you reflect on how you show up in your relationships. This book offers useful tools to help you better understand, connect with, and care for each other.

Day 17

If you have doubts, talk them through with your partner.

Doubts are normal, and every relationship has moments of uncertainty. What matters is what you *do* with those feelings. Bottling up emotions only leads to resentment and distance, while open and honest conversation can build deeper trust and clarity. Your partner isn't a mind reader (even if they somehow *know* you ate the last cookie), so if something's weighing on you, speak up. It might feel uncomfortable at first, but voicing your concerns gives you both a chance to understand, grow, and move forward together. Silence creates space between you; communication builds a bridge.

 Something to talk about: Have you ever had an addiction? If so, what?

Day 18

Get comfortable with forgiveness.

Forgiveness isn't about letting someone off the hook; it's about freeing yourself from the weight of holding on. In relationships, mistakes happen, harsh words are said, and feelings get hurt. Learning how to forgive early helps you move through those moments without letting them build walls between you. It doesn't mean ignoring your feelings or pretending everything's fine. Rather, it's about choosing to work through the hurt instead of keeping score. Forgiveness creates space for healing, growth, and deeper connection. It's not always easy, but it's always worth it, and your relationship will be stronger because of it.

Day 19

The only lust you should be acting on is the lust you have for your partner.

Lust isn't just about people; it's anything that tempts you to step outside the trust of your relationship. It could be flirtation, a fantasy, or even a habit that slowly pulls your attention and affection elsewhere. The truth is what you feed grows. If you're investing time, energy, or emotion into something (or someone) that could harm your connection, it's time to cut the cord. Protecting your relationship means being honest with yourself first. Removing those distractions is about creating space for real intimacy, trust, and long-term joy. Guard what matters most.

 Ask each other: What's a hurt you might still carry that should be discussed?

Day 20

Love is not a sappy feeling; it's putting someone else first.

Love isn't just butterflies and romantic gestures; it's a choice you make, day in and day out. Real love shows up when it's inconvenient or when tempers flare. It's the decision to put someone else's needs before your own, not because you *have* to, but because you *choose* to. That doesn't mean losing yourself or ignoring your own needs; it means choosing partnership over pride and care over convenience. The warm, fuzzy feelings are great, but they're the bonus. The foundation? That's built on showing up, giving grace, and putting each other first, especially when it's hard.

Day 21

Come up with silly nicknames for each other.

Cute nicknames might seem cheesy to outsiders, but inside a relationship, they're like private little hugs wrapped in words. Whether it's "babe," "honey," "peanut," "HB" or something wildly original, like "pookie snuggleface," these nicknames create a sense of intimacy and playfulness. They're small reminders that your connection isn't just about logistics and to-do lists, it's more about affection, familiarity, and fun. Sprinkling in those sweet names can soften challenging moments and add warmth to everyday life. A little silliness goes a long way in keeping love light and fun.

 Conversation starter: Are there any old habits we should leave behind?

Day 22

*In your relationship, spend twice as much time
and half as much money.*

When it comes to building a strong relationship, time beats money every time. Fancy dinners and extravagant gifts are fun, but they can't replace the value of quality time such as talking, laughing, listening, and just *being* together. It's in the unhurried walks, the shared meals at home, and the late-night chats that real connection grows. Spending twice as much time and half as much money shifts the focus from impressing each other to *investing* in each other. Relationships aren't built on receipts; they're built on presence, patience, and shared experiences. So, save a little cash, grab your partner's hand, and make time the most valuable thing you give.

Day 23

Secrets will plague you.

Secrets have a way of weighing down a relationship, even if they're small. That tight feeling in your chest? That's your conscience tapping you on the shoulder. When you're hiding something, it creates distance and an emotional space where connection used to be. It might feel easier to keep it to yourself, but unspoken truths have a way of growing in the dark. Bringing it into the open might be uncomfortable, even scary, but it's also the first step toward healing, rebuilding trust, and lightening your load. Honesty invites honesty. And once it's out, you'll breathe easier.

 Something to talk about: How much time do you think we will spend with each of our parents?

Day 24

Your partner may not be perfect, but they should be perfect for you.

There's no such thing as a flawless partner. But the right person for *you*? That's a different story. They won't check every box or always say the right thing, but they'll balance, challenge, and support you. They will also bring out your best, even on your grumpiest days. A perfect-for-you partner sees your quirks, flaws and weird snack habits, and loves you not despite them, but because of them. It's less about perfection and more about compatibility, shared values, and growing together. Don't chase the ideal, appreciate the real, especially when it fits just right.

Day 25

Be your partner's best friend; the kind you want for yourself.

At the heart of every strong relationship is a solid friendship, the kind where you feel safe, seen, and supported. Being each other's best friend means cheering each other on, sharing inside jokes, and being honest, even when it's hard. It's about being the kind of friend *you* would want; loyal, kind, forgiving, and fun to be around. Romance is necessary, but it's friendship that keeps things steady when life gets messy. Laugh often, listen well, and show up with the same care you'd give your closest friend. That kind of love lasts.

 Finish this sentence: When someone is wrong, they should...

Day 26

You've got to love and accept yourself first.

A strong relationship starts with a strong sense of self. If you don't know who you are, what you value, need, and love, it's all too easy to lose yourself in someone else. Being your own person isn't selfish; it's essential. When you're grounded in who *you* are, you bring your best self into the relationship, not looking to be completed, but ready to share a whole life. Two people who are confident in themselves can build something real, balanced, and lasting. So, take the time to know and love yourself first; it's the best foundation for loving someone else.

Day 27

When in doubt, take the next right step.

Relationships aren't built in sweeping gestures; they grow one small step at a time. When you're unsure what to do, whether it's after a disagreement, during a big life change, or in a quiet season, don't freeze or wait for the "perfect" move. Just take the next small step. Send the text. Ask the question. Offer a hug. Even the tiniest effort keeps the connection moving forward. Doubt feeds on inaction, but progress, no matter how slow, builds trust and clarity. Love doesn't need a grand plan. Sometimes it simply asks you to keep showing up, one small choice at a time.

 Something to talk about: Are there any quirks or odd habits that might become challenging down the road?

Day 28

*Enjoy being engaged for at least six months
before you get married.*

An engagement isn't just a countdown to a wedding; it's a critical time for building a strong foundation on which you'll build your marriage. Allowing at least six months gives you time to truly see how you navigate decisions, stress, and compromise as a team. You learn not just how to plan a wedding, but how to prepare for a *marriage*. It's time to talk about money, family, conflict, and values. These are the things that show up long after the honeymoon ends. Rushing can skip over conversations that matter. Taking your time doesn't mean dragging your feet; it means making sure you're building on solid ground.

Day 29

Before you get married, know if your spouse snores.

Knowing if your future spouse snores is one of those small, yet surprisingly important details. Love may be blind, but sleep deprivation is not. Sharing a bed every night means you'll quickly learn each other's sleep habits, and a surprise snorer can turn "'til death do us part" into "it's 3 a.m. and I'm sleeping on the couch." It's not a deal-breaker, but it's worth discussing. Can it be fixed? Can you laugh about it? Can you sleep through it? Marriage is full of compromises, and sleep might be the first one you make.

 Finish this sentence: The biggest relationship mistake I've made was...

Day 30

*If you have concerns about your relationship,
talk it through before you say, "I do."*

It's normal to have questions or moments of uncertainty before marriage; what matters is whether you talk about them. Ignoring your doubts won't make them disappear; it'll just delay their impact. Instead of bottling things up or brushing them off, sit down with your partner and be honest with each other. Your partner can't help fix a problem they don't know exists. Talking through concerns now is an investment in your future because clarity before commitment is always the smart move.

Day 31

*If you want to see how patient your partner is,
watch them when the power and internet go out.*

Nothing reveals someone's true character quite like the loss of power and internet. Lost internet is the ultimate test of patience, frustration tolerance, and problem-solving under pressure. It's basically a mini simulation of real-life marriage challenges. Watch how your partner reacts when the power goes out, or Netflix won't load. Do they laugh it off, then grab a flashlight and a deck of cards to stay entertained? Do they spiral into dramatic despair? Observe how they handle things when life doesn't go as planned. Because in marriage, things *will* go wrong; what matters is how you respond.

 Conversation starter: When things go wrong, how well do we handle them?

Day 32

Don't marry for any other reason than love.

Marriage is a lifelong partnership, not a solution, a status upgrade, or a checklist item. If love isn't the reason at the core, everything else, such as comfort, timing, pressure, even good intentions, will eventually fall short. Love is what carries you through the hard days, the boring routines, and the unexpected challenges. It's what makes you want to keep showing up, even when it's tough. Without it, you're building a life on shaky ground. Don't marry because it's "time," or because it's convenient; marry because your heart is all in. Love may not solve everything, but it's the only reason that lasts.

Day 33

Marry the person you can't live without.

There's a big difference between someone you *can* live with and someone you *don't want to live without*. The first might check the boxes, keep the peace, and fit neatly into your life, but the second? They *change* your life. They're the ones whose absence you *feel*, whose presence makes the ordinary extraordinary. Marriage is too big, too deep, and too full of unknowns to settle for "good enough." You want the person who challenges you, supports you, makes you laugh when you'd rather cry, and whose love feels like home. That's not just compatibility; it's connection the you've waited for.

 Something to talk about: What makes me the person you can't live without?

Day 34

Don't settle... compromise.

Settling might keep you comfortable, but it won't keep you fulfilled. Choosing a life partner is one of the biggest decisions you'll ever make, and it deserves honesty with them and with yourself. That doesn't mean expecting perfection, but it *does* mean being clear on what truly matters to you: shared values, emotional safety, mutual respect, and the kind of connection that doesn't feel like work every single day. If you find yourself constantly justifying, compromising your core needs, or hoping they'll "change eventually," take a step back. The right person won't require you to shrink or settle, they'll inspire you to grow.

Day 35

Drop your old baggage before you walk down the aisle.

Emotional baggage from the past can quietly influence how you show up in your current relationship. Before you walk down the aisle, take the time to unpack it. That means addressing past hurts, insecurities, or unresolved issues so they don't sneak into your new chapter. Marriage isn't a magic eraser; it's a mirror. And whatever you haven't dealt with will likely surface eventually. Do the work now so you can start your marriage with a clean slate and a clear heart.

 Ask each other: What is something from the past that needs to be resolved before our wedding day? What is the plan?

Day 36

Handle debt as a couple.

Money is one of the top stressors in marriage, so it's important to be united in tackling debt. Instead of playing the blame game or hiding your spending, sit down and make a plan together. Talk openly about your financial habits, goals, and fears. Whether you're paying off loans or climbing out of credit card debt, teamwork makes the difference. Debt doesn't disappear overnight and approaching it as a shared mission can strengthen your bond rather than break it. Celebrate small wins along the way, because progress feels sweeter when you're chasing freedom together.

Day 37

If a relationship must be a secret, you shouldn't be in it.

If your relationship must be kept in the shadows, it's time to ask why. Secrets and hiding aren't signs of passion; they're red warning lights. Love should make you feel safe, proud, and seen, not like you have to explain it away or tiptoe around it. And this goes beyond just the two of you. If someone outside your relationship, whether it's an ex, a "friend," or a so-called secret someone, has to be kept quiet, that's a problem, too. Any connection that requires lies or loopholes to maintain doesn't belong in a healthy relationship. If something or someone needs to stay hidden, it might be time to shine a light on what you're really building and who you're building it with.

 Conversation Starter: What are our outstanding debts?

Day 38

Know what your partner considers a big purchase.

Money can be one of the hottest topics in a marriage. What feels like "no big deal" to you might feel huge to them, and those differences can spark unnecessary tension. Talk about it now: What dollar amount requires a conversation? How do you each decide what's worth splurging on? Understanding each other's comfort zones with spending is about showing respect and avoiding surprises that lead to arguments later. When you know how your partner views finances, you can make decisions as a team, reduce stress, and keep money from becoming a wedge in your relationship.

Day 39

Get to the root of any jealousy.

Jealousy is like a warning light; it tells you something's off, but it's up to you to figure out what. Instead of letting it fester, lashing out, or—worse—ignoring it, take a step back and ask yourself where it's really coming from. Is it insecurity? A gap in communication? A past wound that hasn't fully healed? Once you've named the root, bring it to your partner with honesty, not blame. Say, "Here's what I'm feeling, and here's why I think it's showing up." Jealousy handled with curiosity and maturity can deepen your connection and build trust. Left unchecked, though, it becomes a silent wedge, chipping away at closeness. Don't fear it alone; face it together.

 Something to talk about: What do you consider a big purchase?

Day 40

Be clear on your must-haves and can't stands in your relationship.

Everyone has things they deeply value and things they absolutely can't live with. Knowing your must-haves and can't-stands isn't picky, it's smart. When you're clear on what truly matters to you in a relationship, it's easier to recognize whether your partner aligns with your values. Don't minimize your non-negotiables to avoid conflict. Clarity now saves heartbreak later, and it helps ensure you're building a future that actually fits *you*.

Day 41

Act on deal-breakers immediately.

When a deal-breaker shows up in a relationship, don't sweep it under the rug and hope it disappears, because it won't. Ignoring it only breeds resentment and distance. Whether it's about finances, values, fidelity, or lifestyle, confronting it head-on is crucial. The action step? Name it out loud. Sit down with your partner, clearly express what feels non-negotiable, and listen to their perspective. Then work together to find a resolution, set boundaries, or make a plan. Some topics are simply too complex to handle alone. Don't be afraid to get professional help in the form of a marriage or relationship counselor if needed. Addressing deal-breakers early protects your relationship from bigger fractures later.

 Ask each other: What are your marriage deal-breakers?

Day 42

*Make sure you are both on the same page
regarding kids, sex, and money.*

Before getting married, it's crucial to have open conversations about the big stuff: kids, money, and sex are three biggies, but there are others too, such as religion and politics. These aren't just topics; they're cornerstones of a shared life. Misaligned expectations in these areas can lead to resentment and disconnection over time. Talk early, talk honestly, and keep talking as you grow. Being on the same page now helps you face the future with unity, rather than surprise or frustration.

Day 43

*Marriage doesn't solve relationship problems,
it magnifies them.*

If you're hoping marriage will fix the cracks in your relationship, think again. Marriage doesn't erase problems; it puts them under a microscope. The things you're brushing off now will only get louder when life gets more complicated. From finances to family dynamics, pressure tends to amplify what's already there. That's why it's so important to address issues *before* you walk down the aisle. A strong marriage begins with honesty, self-awareness, and a willingness to grow, not wishful thinking.

 Ask each other: What are the best and worst traits each of us inherited from our parents?

Day 44

Marry someone you love talking with.

Looks fade, hobbies change, but meaningful conversation? That's a forever kind of glue. As time passes, you'll spend more time just talking about your day, your dreams, your worries, and the grocery list. And in those quiet moments, you'll want a partner who listens well, speaks kindly, and truly gets you. Marrying someone you love to talk to means you'll always have a teammate, a sounding board, and a friend, even when the rest of life gets noisy. When you keep learning and experiencing new things as a couple, you naturally spark deeper, more engaging conversations. Shared curiosity keeps your dialogue fresh, turning even ordinary evenings into moments of connection that strengthen your bond over the years.

Day 45

Your engagement ring loves spa treatments, too!

Your engagement ring may symbolize eternal love, but it still needs regular TLC to keep it shining like the day you said, "Yes." Your ring collects more lotion, crumbs, and gunk than you'd expect, so give it a spa day now and then. A simple soak in warm water with a drop of gentle dish soap, followed by a soft-bristled toothbrush scrub, will do wonders. Rinse thoroughly, pat it dry, and voilà, the sparkle restored! Alternatively, you can take it to a jeweler for a professional cleaning and check-up a few times a year.

 Finish this sentence: Past relationships have taught me...

Day 46

*Be honest about who you are and what you
want before you say, "I do."*

A strong marriage is built on trust and transparency from the very beginning. Share your values, your goals, and your non-negotiables openly so you both know exactly what you're committing to. When you're upfront about what matters most to you, and invite your partner to do the same, you lay the groundwork for a relationship that's rooted in mutual respect. Love grows best in the light, not in hidden agendas. Starting your marriage with honesty ensures you're both saying "yes" to the same future, with eyes and hearts wide open.

Day 47

*Talk about the important things before you
commit to marriage.*

Before saying "I do," make sure you've said *a lot* about the stuff that really matters. Topics like money, kids, family, values, and faith aren't just deep, they're necessary. These conversations may not be the most fun, but they help you see if you're aligned or heading in different directions. You don't have to agree on everything, but you do need to know where you stand and how you'll handle differences. Avoiding these talks now might feel easier, but facing them early will save you a world of confusion later.

 Conversation starter: Are there any areas where you feel insecure about our relationship?

Day 48

The best gifts you can give are time, attention, and love.

In a world full of distractions and noise, the most meaningful thing you can give your partner is your undivided attention. Time spent together, focus that says, "I see you," and love that's consistent and kind are the real treasures. It's about the daily choice to show up, listen, and care. The little moments, like checking in, holding hands, or making space for each other, often mean more than anything money can buy.

Day 49

Whoever you were as a single person will only be magnified once you're married.

If you're generous, kind, and self-aware as a single person, those qualities will often grow deeper in partnership. But if you avoid conflict, for example, marriage can make that tendency even more pronounced. You might find yourself staying silent during important conversations or letting resentment build instead of addressing issues. Recognizing the pattern now gives you a chance to work on it. Whether it's learning healthy communication skills, practicing speaking up, or addressing old fears around disagreement, the inner work you do before marriage lays the foundation for a stronger bond. A healthy relationship thrives when both people bring their best, most honest selves to the table and stay committed to growing from there.

 Finish this sentence: What I fear most about marriage is...

Day 50

Passionate friends make the best couples.

Romance may spark the flame, but friendship keeps it burning. The best marriages are rooted in deep, passionate friendship, the kind where you feel safe, seen, and genuinely enjoyed. You laugh together, support each other's dreams, and stick around when things get hard. It's not about being perfect partners, it's about being loyal teammates who love each other fiercely, flaws and all. Passion fades within moments, but friendship holds strong throughout the years.

Day 51

Just because you get engaged doesn't mean you should rush to set a wedding date.

Just because you get engaged doesn't mean you need to slap a date on the calendar before the champagne bubbles settle. Engagement isn't just a countdown; it's a season all on its own. A time to savor, to talk through the big stuff, and to make sure you're building something solid before diving into planning centerpieces and seating charts. Rushing to "I do" might mean skipping the critical "do you..." conversations, such as how you handle money, in-laws, and whether you're a dog or cat person. The wedding will be one day. Your marriage? That's the forever part. Take your time, enjoy the glow, and build a solid foundation. Because forever deserves better.

 Ask each other: How long should we stay engaged? Why?

Day 52

Your partner will not be perfect... just perfect-ish for you.

Perfection is a myth, especially in relationships. Real love begins when we stop searching for flawlessness and start embracing humanity. It's about seeing someone's strengths, messiness, and quirks clearly, and loving them not in spite of it, but because of it. Learning to love someone's imperfections with tenderness and respect is what turns affection into something lasting and true. In the end, it's the imperfect pieces that make your love story one-of-a-kind. Choosing each other, flaws and all, is what makes a marriage not just real, but beautiful.

Day 53

Read The 5 Love Languages by Gary Chapman

Before you say, "I do," say, "I get you." *The 5 Love Languages* by Gary Chapman is a classic relationship book for a reason: it helps you understand how you and your partner give and receive love. Are you a words-of-affirmation person paired with someone who shows love through acts of service? No wonder things feel off! Reading this book together sparks "aha" moments and real conversations. You'll learn to love smarter, not harder.

Bonus idea: Plan a date night around each love language.

 Something to talk about: What is your love language? Why do you think that is?

Day 54

Appreciate how lucky you are to find each other.

You didn't just *find* each other, you chose each other in a world full of almosts, not-quites, and swipe-lefts. That's pretty magical. It's easy to get caught up in the planning, the Pinterest boards, and the opinions flying at you from every direction. But don't forget to pause and feel the importance of this rare, beautiful thing: two people who see each other clearly and still say, "Yes, I'm in." Appreciate that and let gratitude be the common theme in your relationship, not just something you express in a thank-you note after the wedding. You're not just lucky to have love, you're lucky to have *this* love, right here, right now. Don't take it for granted.

Day 55

Create a few playlists for special occasions.

Create a few playlists now that will become the soundtrack of your story later. One for road trips, one for cozy nights in, one for cooking dinner together, and yes, one for making up after a fight. Music has a sneaky way of locking in memories, shifting moods, and saying what words sometimes can't. Years from now, you'll hear *that* song and be instantly transported to your first tiny apartment or that rainy Sunday you danced barefoot in the kitchen. Playlists are more than background noise; they're the soundtrack to your life together.

 Ask each other: Do we need to agree on our core religious and political beliefs?

Day 56

Get to the root of your wants and needs and understand the difference.

Wants are surface level things you *think* will make you happy. Needs are deeper, non-negotiables that support your emotional well-being. In relationships, knowing the difference is key. You might want daily text messages, but what you really *need* is to feel connected. Clarifying what's essential versus what's nice to have helps you communicate more effectively and build a healthier, more balanced relationship. When you understand your needs clearly, you stop chasing perfection and start nurturing connection rooted in what truly matters.

Day 57

Train yourself to let go of everything you fear losing.

Attachment rooted in fear leads to control, anxiety, and the exhausting need to hold on tight. But love that flows from trust and inner peace is far more liberating, for both you and your partner. Letting go doesn't mean you care less; it means you trust enough to release the grip and let love breathe. Fear says, "Don't let go or you'll lose them." Wisdom says, "Loosen your hold so they can choose to stay." When you stop living in fear of loss, you begin living in the fullness of now. And presence—not pressure—is where real love thrives. Letting go isn't about giving up; it's about showing up without fear clouding the connection.

 Conversation starter: Do you prefer city or suburbs?

Day 58

Love is not about possession; it's about appreciation.

Love isn't about staking a claim; it's about seeing, valuing, and celebrating who your partner truly is. It's not "you're mine," rather it's, "I'm lucky to walk through life with you." Possession tries to control; appreciation lets love breathe. When you love with appreciation, you admire their quirks, support their dreams, and honor their individuality, even when it doesn't revolve around you. That kind of love builds trust, not tension. Say thank you often, notice the little things, and be their biggest fan.

Day 59

Watch how your partner treats dogs, old people, and breakfast waitresses.

Watch how your partner treats those who can't offer much in return. Kindness isn't just in grand gestures; it's in the small, unguarded moments. Do they smile at the server who got the order wrong? Help the elderly neighbor with her groceries? Notice if they step in without being asked, not for praise but simply because it's the right thing to do. Do they kneel to pet a stranger's dog like it's an old friend? These glimpses reveal character more than sweet words ever could. Pay attention. Marriage isn't built on date nights and filtered selfies, it's built on decency, empathy, and how they act when no one's watching (or when the coffee's late).

 Ask each other: How do you each feel about adoption? (pets and children)

Day 60

Pick a wedding date that's easy to remember.

It may sound small, but remembering your anniversary is a quiet, powerful way of saying, "I see us. I value us." Life will get crowded with jobs, kids, bills, and endless to-do lists, but your relationship needs regular moments of celebration, too. Forgetting once might not be a dealbreaker, but making a habit of overlooking milestones can chip away at connection over time. Some couples choose a date that overlaps with a holiday or another special occasion. The upside? It's easier to remember, and you can sometimes fold the celebrations together for a bigger impact. The downside? Your anniversary may end up competing for attention or being shared with extended family instead of being kept between the two of you. Choose what makes sense for both of you.

Day 61

Lay a foundation of friendship with your future in-laws.

Marriage is a union of two people, and often, two families. You don't have to be best friends with your in-laws, but building a foundation of mutual respect and kindness goes a long way. Take time to learn what matters to them. Be curious, not critical. Find common ground and shared laughter. This friendship isn't just for holidays, it's for life. The smoother the relationship with your in-laws, the more peaceful and supported your marriage will feel. Treat them like an extension of your partner, not a rival, but a relationship worth nurturing.

 Something to talk about: How do you imagine celebrating our anniversary?

Marriage is less about finding the right person and more about becoming the right partner.

Chapter 2

Dreams, Details, and Decisions
Your fairytale needs a plan

Day 62

Your wedding day is not about pleasing everyone else.

Your wedding day is not about pleasing everyone else; it's about celebrating *your* love, *your* story, and the commitment *you* are making. It's easy to get swept up in the opinions, expectations, and traditions others may want to impose, whether it's your seating chart, your guest list, or what flavor the cake "should" be. But trying to make everyone happy is the fastest way to forget what the day is truly about: the two of you.

This is your one shot to design a day that feels like *you*. If you want a donut wall instead of a tiered cake, or to walk down the aisle to your favorite 80s ballad, do it! If you want bridesmen instead of bridesmaids, do it! The people who love you will support the choices that reflect your happiness, not just their preferences. At the end of the day, you won't remember who rolled their eyes at your K9 ring bearer; you'll remember how it felt to marry your partner. So, permit yourself to prioritize joy over approval.

 Conversation Starter: What is something you want to include in our wedding that might not be traditional or expected?

Day 63

Be prepared to compromise.

Marriage is a constant balancing act between two individuals with their own opinions, quirks, and ways of doing things, including loading the dishwasher. You won't always agree, and that's okay. What matters is how you handle the space between your differences. Compromise doesn't mean giving up your voice; it means using it wisely. It's saying, "This matters more to you than it does to me, so I'll give a little here," and trusting that your partner will do the same when the roles reverse. It's less about winning and more about building something that works for *both* of you.

Day 64

Remember sunblock and birth control when
packing for your honeymoon.

Nothing says "welcome to married life" like a surprise sunburn or an unplanned pregnancy. It's easy to get caught up in the excitement and forget the basics, but a little preparation goes a long way. Whether you're lounging on a beach or exploring a new city, you'll want to feel your best, and that means taking care of your skin *and* your plans. These aren't glamorous items, but they're practical, thoughtful, and future you will be grateful. So, throw in that SPF, double-check your method of choice, and get ready to enjoy your first big adventure as a married couple—relaxed, protected, and fully present.

 Ask each other: Do you think arguing is part of every relationship?

Day 65

---

*While planning your wedding, don't forget to
plan for your marriage, too.*

While planning the wedding, don't forget to plan for your marriage, too. You're probably knee-deep in napkin colors and cake tastings, but have you taken time to daydream about your *married* life? The wedding is one beautiful, love-filled blur. But your marriage? That's the long game. You're crafting a future, not just a party. So yes, pick your first dance song, but also picture the quiet Tuesdays, the hard conversations, and the belly laughs ten years in. Imagine the milestones still to come—buying your first home, raising kids if you choose, celebrating silver anniversaries—and how you'll face them together. Don't leave forever to chance. Design it with heart.

Day 66

---

*Plan a decompression day before leaving
for your honeymoon.*

Weddings are beautiful, but let's be honest, they're also exhausting. After all the emotions, logistics, and social energy, your body and mind deserve a moment to rest. Instead of sprinting straight to the airport, give yourself a quiet buffer day. Sleep in. Order takeout. Relive your favorite moments. Breathe. This little window of calm can help you transition from "event mode" to "us mode," and you'll arrive on your honeymoon more rested, present, and able to enjoy the adventure ahead.

 Something to talk about: Do you think it's better to add a decompression day before or after the honeymoon?

Day 67

Don't be stubborn or hard-headed.

Marriage isn't a power struggle; it's a partnership. Digging in your heels to "win" an argument can drive a wedge between you that's harder to fix than whatever the issue was in the first place. Pride might feel good in the moment, but humility fosters deeper connections. Being willing to listen, to admit when you're wrong, and to see things from your partner's point of view is a sign of strength, not weakness. Stubbornness might get the last word, but openness gives you a lasting relationship. Let go of the need to be right and hold onto the goal of being *kind*.

Day 68

Be sure to invite the "right" people to your wedding.

When it comes to the guest list, choose wisely. It isn't about numbers, it's about *meaning*. Who has shown up for your relationship? Who makes you feel celebrated, supported, and safe? Those are the people you want in attendance. Don't invite out of guilt or obligation. Invite with intention. Every face you see on your wedding day should bring a smile, not stress. Quality over quantity every single time. The right guest list creates a special atmosphere where joy flows freely, hugs are real, and your love is witnessed by the people who matter most. Choose wisely.

 Ask each other: Do you think it's more important to have more friends or extended family at our wedding? Why?

Day 69

The little things are often big things in disguise.

It's easy to chase the big milestones like weddings, anniversaries, and vacations, but real love lives in the little moments. It's in shared glances, inside jokes, late-night snacks, or the perfect cup of tea after a long day. These small, everyday interactions often slip by unnoticed, but they're what build a life. Years from now, it won't be the fancy dinner you remember, it will be how your spouse made that perfect cup of tea at the right moment or how you laughed until you cried during a grocery run. Pay attention and treasure the ordinary. One day, you'll realize those small things were the ones that mattered the most.

Day 70

Don't be afraid to make and keep a budget.

Money doesn't need to be a source of stress, but it does need a plan. A budget isn't a restriction; it's a roadmap. It helps you align your values, set shared goals, and avoid the kind of surprises that can lead to tension. Discussing money openly may feel uncomfortable at first, but transparency fosters trust. Budgets give you permission to say "yes" to what matters and "no" without guilt. Whether you're saving for a house or just trying to avoid debt, being on the same page financially is a gift you give to your future.

 Conversation starter: Do you think a financial budget is necessary, optional, or irrelevant?

Day 71

Don't compare your relationship to anyone else's.

It's tempting to measure your relationship against someone else's, especially in a world where highlight reels are everywhere. Comparison is sneaky. It makes you focus on what's missing instead of what's meaningful. Every couple is different, and no one's love story is perfect, no matter how it looks from the outside. Don't rob yourself of joy by wishing your life looked like someone else's. Instead, nurture what's uniquely yours. Celebrate the love, rhythm, and connection that only the two of you share. Gratitude grows stronger when you stop comparing and start appreciating what you have right here, right now.

Day 72

*Don't shoulder too much responsibility
to do things your way.*

It's easy to fall into the trap of thinking, "If I don't do it, it won't get done right." But taking everything on your way can lead to burnout and resentment. A strong partnership isn't about control; it's about collaboration. Share the load. Trust your partner's strengths. Communicate, delegate, and be willing to loosen your grip on the small stuff. When both people feel heard and valued, the relationship thrives. You don't have to carry it all alone; and truthfully, love grows best when you invite your partner to help carry the weight with you.

 Something to talk about: If our love story were a book, what would you want the next chapter to be titled?

Day 73

*Write a letter telling your partner **why** you are choosing to commit your life to them.*

Putting your love into words is a powerful act. A commitment letter isn't just sweet, it's meaningful. It reminds both of you *why* you're choosing this path together. In the rush of wedding planning or everyday life, it's easy to lose sight of the deeper reason behind it all. Taking the time to write a letter that says, "This is what I see in you; this is why I choose you," creates a lasting reminder of the heart behind the promise. Keep it somewhere safe and revisit it when you need to remember the strength of your beginning.

Day 74

Don't get so caught up in planning that you forget to connect with each other.

It's easy to get wrapped up in logistics such as timelines, budgets, and seating charts, but don't let the planning become more important than the person you're marrying. Take intentional breaks to reconnect outside of "wedding mode." Go on dates where you don't talk about the big day. Leave sweet notes. Check in on how the other person is really doing. When stress builds, love can get lost in the shuffle. Keep choosing each other amid the madness. Planning a wedding is temporary. Loving each other is the forever part.

 Ask each other: What family wedding traditions do you feel strongly about?

Day 75

*After your honeymoon, schedule a decompression
day before heading back to work.*

Coming back from a honeymoon is like coming down from a cloud.
Plan for a soft landing rather than diving straight into your inbox
or to-do list. Take one day to unpack, do laundry, and reconnect in
your space before re-entering your work life. That extra time gives
you space to reflect on your trip and ease into the rhythm of your
new normal together. It's a simple gift to yourselves that can make
the return to reality feel less overwhelming and more intentional.

Day 76

*Ask your fiancé which parts of the wedding they
care least about.*

Asking your fiancé which parts of the wedding they care least about
is one of the simplest ways to reduce stress, save time, and avoid
unnecessary disagreements. Maybe they don't have strong
opinions about flowers, place settings, or the type of cake. Knowing
this upfront lets you focus your energy (and budget) where it
matters most to both of you. It also helps you divide tasks in a way
that plays to your strengths and interests, instead of forcing one
another into decision fatigue over details neither of you care about.
Planning a wedding is a team effort, but that doesn't mean each
decision needs equal input. Sometimes the best gift you can give
each other is the freedom to care less about the things that don't
matter to you or your fiancé.

 Something to talk about: What part of
the wedding do you care least about?

Day 77

Ask yourself, "If I were paying for the entire wedding myself, would this vendor or service be so important?"

Weddings get expensive fast, and when someone else is helping foot the bill, it's easy to say "yes" to extras that may not hold much meaning. But before adding another vendor or upgrade, pause and ask: "If I were paying cash for this out of my own pocket, would it matter this much?" This simple gut check can bring clarity and shift your focus back to what really counts. Spend intentionally on things that reflect *your* values as a couple. A meaningful wedding isn't about impressing others; it's about celebrating your love in a way that feels true and thoughtful.

Day 78

No matter how expensive the wedding, it will not make your marriage any stronger.

You can spend $5,000 or $50,000 on a wedding, but the price tag won't determine the strength of your marriage. What matters most isn't the venue, the gown, or the gourmet meal; it's the foundation you're building together. Beautiful décor can't fix broken communication, and over-the-top cakes don't replace trust. A simple ceremony full of sincerity and love will always outshine a lavish one lacking connection. So, plan the celebration you want, but don't equate expense with importance.

 Conversation starter: What wedding splurge do you feel is worth the cost? Which ones aren't?

Day 79

Don't be afraid to pause if things get out of control.

Planning a wedding can stir up all kinds of pressure, like family expectations, budget battles, or endless details. If things start spiraling or you feel overwhelmed, it's okay to call a time-out. Step back. Breathe. Regroup. Your mental and emotional health matter more than sticking to a timeline or pleasing everyone. Taking a pause doesn't mean you're failing; it means you're choosing peace over panic. Whether it's a ten-minute walk or a week away from planning, giving yourselves space to reset can help you return with clarity and calmness.

Day 80

Don't lose your fiancé in the planning.

It's ironic how a celebration meant to unite you can sometimes pull you apart. Wedding planning gets busy fast with checklists, deadlines, and opinions flying from all directions. In the flurry, don't forget what it's all about: the person standing beside you. Make space for connection outside the planning. Go on non-wedding dates. Check in with each other and share a laugh. Your relationship should always come first, because when the music fades and the guests leave, it's just the two of you. Stay connected. Stay present. While the wedding is one day, the marriage is the real celebration.

 Something to talk about: Should we elope or have a small backyard wedding?

Day 81

*Don't expect your partner to be super-excited
about every wedding detail.*

Not everyone dreams about flower arrangements or cake tastings, and that's okay. If your partner isn't jumping up and down about linen colors or invitation fonts, don't take it personally. It doesn't mean they care less about the wedding; it just means they may show their enthusiasm in different ways. Focus on what they do care about, then listen and respect their desires for that aspect of the day. Planning works best when you each play to your strengths and styles. Let the balance be a blessing, not a frustration.

Day 82

Don't panic about "forever, till death do us part".

The idea of *forever* can feel huge, even intimidating. But here's the truth: you don't have to figure out forever today. You just have to show up for this day, and then the next. It's about one choice and one day at a time. Marriage isn't a sprint to the finish; it's a slow, steady walk-through life together. Take the pressure off. You're not expected to know how it all unfolds, just to be present, honest, and committed to growing together. Forever isn't made in one vow, it's made in daily love, forgiveness, and the decision to keep showing up. And when you look back years from now, you'll see that forever was built in the little moments all along.

 Conversation starter: What are your thoughts on traditional wedding vows? Which parts do you like, which parts do you not agree with?

Day 83

Take inspiration from other people's weddings.

Your wedding isn't a competition; it's your story, your inside jokes, your shared songs, and your style. You don't need to "outdo" anyone else's wedding, but you can take inspiration from memorable moments you've seen, then make them your own. Forget trends and focus on what feels true to you. The best weddings aren't the flashiest; they're the ones that reflect your personality and values. Whether it's barefoot on a beach or a backyard potluck, the meaning behind it matters most. Skip the pressure to impress and create a day that feels unmistakably yours. That's the kind of celebration people remember, especially you and your partner.

Day 84

Planning shouldn't be all stress.

Wedding planning can feel like a full-time job with flowers and tears. But don't let checklists steal your joy. Pause for the sweet stuff. Laugh at the ridiculous decisions (why are there 37 napkin colors?!). Savor the cake tasting. Dance in your living room when the playlist hits. This is your story, not just the wedding, but the lead-up. The best memories might come from the planning, not just the ceremony itself. Remember to stop, breathe, and enjoy the ride. After all, that's often where the magic happens.

 Ask each other: What was the best wedding you've been to? What made it special?

Day 85

Leave copies of your honeymoon itinerary and passports with a trusted friend.

Travel plans can get derailed in an instant by missed connections, lost luggage, or stolen bags. If anything goes sideways, having a backup plan (and someone back home who knows your schedule) is priceless. Share your itinerary and copies of essential documents with a trusted friend or family member. Include hotel numbers, flight times, and emergency contacts. It's one of those things you hope never gets used, but you'll be glad you did it if trouble arises. A little preparation gives you peace of mind, so you can focus on enjoying every minute together.

Day 86

Don't let a smooth-talking salesperson blow your wedding budget.

There will always be someone trying to convince you that "just one more upgrade" will make your day perfect. It won't. Perfection doesn't come from the highest price tag, it comes from love, joy, and shared moments. Be wise. Stick to your budget. Question every purchase with "Do we *really* need this?" and "Will we remember this five years from now?" Don't let pressure or panic talk you into debt. You're building a life, not just a wedding day. Save your money for adventures, not chair sashes.

 Conversation starter: What is a code word we can use when someone is encouraging us to blow the budget?

Day 87

Weddings can bring out the best and worst in people.

Weddings are beautiful, but they are also emotional landmines. People get stressed. Expectations collide. Old family dynamics resurface. It's not personal, it's human. If tensions rise, choose grace. If someone disappoints you, assume good intent. This is a big day, but it's also a *big ask* of the people around you. Be patient. Be kind. And when possible, forgive quickly. You'll feel lighter. Protect your peace as if it were part of the ceremony. Because in the end, the real win isn't just getting through the day, it's doing it with your relationships intact. Love big. Breathe deep. And maybe pack a little extra patience in your pocket.

Day 88

Weddings last a day... the marriage lasts a lifetime.

Weddings last a day, but the marriage lasts a lifetime. It's easy to get swept up in the excitement of planning with the flowers, the music, and the outfits, but the real celebration begins after the party ends. The vows you exchange are bigger than a single moment and become the foundation of every tomorrow you share. Long after the cake is eaten and the photos are tucked away, what matters most is how you show up for each other day after day. A wedding is a beautiful beginning, but it is just that, the beginning. The true joy comes from building a marriage filled with trust, laughter, and love that grows stronger with time.

 Something to talk about: How can we be sure to slow down and enjoy our special day?

Day 89

Have a toast in your back pocket, just in case
you feel inspired to share.

Even if you're not the speech-giving type, have a few words ready in case inspiration hits. Emotions run high on wedding days, and you might find yourself inspired by the room, the love, or the overwhelming joy of finally getting to this moment. Write down a few thoughts ahead of time. Thank the people who helped make it happen. Speak directly to your partner. It doesn't need to be perfect, just personal. A simple, heartfelt toast can be more powerful than any choreographed performance. And even if you don't end up saying it aloud, you'll be glad you had it in your heart.

Day 90

Break in new shoes far in advance of the wedding.

Break in your wedding shoes *well* before the big day, your feet (and your mood) will thank you. Those gorgeous heels or polished dress shoes might look perfect, but if they haven't been worn in, they can quickly turn into torture devices by hour two. Blisters, pinched toes, or sore arches are not the kind of memories you want to carry into your marriage. Wear them around the house, dance in them in the kitchen, and take a few laps around the block. Get your feet used to them and keep a comfy backup pair nearby just in case. You'll be on your feet dancing and making memories, and the last thing you want is to be limping through your "happily ever after."

 Ask each other: Who do you want (and not want) to give a toast at the wedding?

Day 91

Plan an after-party.

Once the official festivities wrap, the real fun often begins. An after-party doesn't have to be extravagant. It's that relaxed, laugh-till-you-cry moment with your inner circle where the pressure is off, the cake has been cut, and you can finally let loose. Whether it's a rooftop lounge, a backyard fire pit, or just grabbing hotel lobby snacks in sweatpants, make space for the celebration to keep flowing. Decide ahead of time if you want to spread the word to all your guests or keep it to a small, intimate group of best friends because this changes the vibe entirely. Either way, an after-party gives you the chance to soak it in, unwind, and create memories you wouldn't have otherwise enjoyed. You only get one wedding night, so why not stretch the joy and let it last a little longer?

Day 92

Create a special "getting ready" playlist.

The morning of your wedding sets the tone for the entire day. The perfect playlist can work wonders for your energy, nerves, and mindset. Choose songs that make you feel confident, nostalgic, loved, and lighthearted. Include favorites that remind you of your relationship, and don't forget a few dance-in-your-robe tunes to get everyone smiling. Music can calm nerves and lift anxious hearts. It becomes the backdrop to your pre-wedding rituals, something you'll always remember when those songs come on again.

 Finish this sentence: The perfect after-party is....

Day 93

Don't underestimate a well-stocked emergency kit!!

Trust me: something unexpected will happen. A button will pop, a zipper will stick, someone will get a blister, and tissues will be needed. Enter: the emergency kit. Fill it with Band-Aids, bobby pins, safety pins, a mini sewing kit, stain remover, floss, breath mints, and deodorant. Toss in pain relievers, snacks, and anything else that'll save the day quietly and quickly. You may not use it all, but you'll be grateful to have it the *one* time you need it. Being prepared means fewer panic moments and more peace.

Day 94

Be realistic about the guest list.

Guest lists can be one of the biggest stressors in wedding planning. There's pressure from family, work friends, long-lost cousins... but here's the truth: you don't owe everyone an invite. Your wedding is about love, not obligation. Focus on the people who have shown up for your relationship, such as those who lift you, support you, and genuinely want to be there. It's okay to keep it intimate. It's okay to set boundaries. You're not planning a reunion; you're celebrating a sacred promise. Choose your people with care, and you'll create a space that feels joyful, peaceful, and full of love. And remember, the energy in the room matters more than the number of chairs you fill. The right guest list creates the kind of atmosphere where your love story can truly shine.

 Conversation starter: Who are your top priority guests, and who should be on the optional list?

Day 95

Ask your wedding venue for vendor recommendations.

Your venue isn't just a location, it's a resource. They've hosted dozens (if not hundreds) of weddings and know which vendors consistently deliver quality and work well under pressure. Before you start your internet deep dive, ask for their short list. They may have partnerships or packages that save you time and stress. It also helps ensure your team is familiar with the space, which can make your day flow smoothly. Leverage your vendors' experience because it's part of what you're paying for. And the more your vendors know each other, the better your day will run.

Day 96

Consider a separate email address for all wedding planning correspondence.

Wedding planning comes with a digital avalanche—quotes, contracts, RSVPs, confirmations, you name it. If you don't want your inbox to implode, create a dedicated wedding email. Use it for all vendor communication, sign-ups, and planning tools. It keeps everything organized and easy to search. Plus, it helps you both stay on the same page if you share access. And after the wedding? You can retire the inbox like a time capsule of your planning journey. Smart, simple, and future-you will thank you when you don't miss that final cake tasting reminder buried under work emails.

 Ask each other: Who is the more organized one in our relationship?

Day 97

Do you want quality or quantity for the invitation list?

It's tempting to invite everyone you've ever met to your wedding, but here's the truth: the bigger the guest list, the less face time you'll actually have with anyone. With large weddings, the day becomes a blur of quick hugs, rushed greetings, and mental notes to circle back (that you never will). If meaningful moments matter more to you than headcount, consider scaling back. Smaller doesn't mean less special—it means more *connected*. You'll remember who you laughed with, cried with, and danced with, not just who signed the guest book. Quality beats quantity every time.

Day 98

Let your personality, not expectations, inspire the day.

It's easy to get swept into what a wedding "should" look like, what family expects, what social media encourages, and what tradition dictates. But this is *your* day. Let it reflect your personality, love story, and what matters most. Strip away the pressure to impress or conform. Want tacos instead of steak? Do it! Want to make your first dance a rock ballad? Go for it! The best weddings feel authentic because they *are*. When you plan from the heart instead of from obligation, you'll create a day that's not only memorable, but meaningful.

 Something to talk about: Do you feel it's necessary to speak to each guest individually on our wedding day?

Day 99

Eliminate the poison of unrealistic expectations.

Let's be honest: perfection is a myth. Something will go off-script— a flower arrangement will wilt, someone will run late, or a song might skip, but none of that will ruin your day unless you let it. Unrealistic expectations set you up for disappointment, not joy. Choose grace over perfection. Expect a little chaos and laugh through it. Focus on love, not logistics. Your wedding doesn't need to be flawless to be unforgettable. It just needs to be full of heart. Let go of "perfect" so you can fully enjoy "real." Years from now, it's often the unplanned moments that you'll remember most, the ones that bring laughter and stories you'll tell over and over.

Day 100

Respect how your partner handles bad moods and disappointments.

Everyone processes stress and disappointment differently. Some retreat, some vent, some need space, others need hugs. You don't have to *fix* your partner's tough days; you just need to respect how they work through them. Ask what helps. Give grace when they need to shut down or when emotions spill over. Love isn't just about enjoying someone at their best; it's also about understanding them at their most human. When you honor their coping style (even if it's different from yours), you're building emotional safety, and that's the bedrock of a lasting relationship.

 Conversation starter: Be honest, are there any areas of unrealistic expectation for our wedding day?

Day 101

Learn to speak your spouse's Love Language.

Everyone gives and receives love differently. For some, it's through words. For others, it's gifts, time, acts of service, or touch. Knowing your partner's love language helps you love them in a way they truly *feel*. If you're giving gifts but they need words, your efforts may miss the mark, not for lack of trying, but for lack of translation. Take time to learn their language. Speak it fluently. It's not about changing who you are; it's about showing love in the way they understand best. Connection thrives when both partners feel deeply seen and appreciated.

Day 102

If you have any hesitation, now is the time to determine why.

If you have any hesitation about marriage, now is the time to pay attention, not to panic, but to get curious. Doubt doesn't always mean "don't", sometimes it just means "dig deeper." Are you nervous about losing independence? Unsure about how you'll handle conflict? Concerned about mismatched values or expectations? Hesitation is a signal, not a stop sign. Listen to it with honesty and courage. Talk it through, ask hard questions, and get clear on what's behind the hesitation. The strongest marriages aren't built on blind certainty, they're built on truth, self-awareness, and the willingness to face discomfort before it turns into regret.

 Finish this sentence: I believe the keys to a strong marriage are...

Day 103

Establish a budget, then stick to it!

Money stress can creep into even the most joyful planning. Set a clear, realistic budget—regardless of whether your parents are paying for the wedding or if you are. Be honest about what you can afford. Prioritize what really matters to *you*. Once your budget is set, protect it. Boundaries with spending mean more peace, fewer regrets, and a smoother start to your marriage. It's not about cutting corners, it's about cutting stress. A thoughtful, intentional celebration is just as meaningful (and often more beautiful) than one that breaks the bank.

Tip: Pad your budget with a "surprise fund" of five to 10 percent for last minute unexpected costs.

Day 104

Prioritize and strategize your photo list.

The day will fly by, but your photos will last forever. Sit down before the big day and decide to capture what *really* matters: family shots, quiet moments, or fun candid shots. Don't just rely on your photographer's instincts; communicate your wants clearly. Create a list of must-have groupings and special details that you don't want to miss. Share it with a trusted friend or planner who can help wrangle people when it's go-time. That way, you can focus on smiling, not searching for Uncle Bob. Well-planned photos tell the full story. Years from now, you'll be grateful for every frame.

 Ask each other: Which wedding day photos are the most important to you?

Day 105

Don't skip your final dress fitting.

Don't leave this one to chance. A last-minute wardrobe surprise is no one's idea of fun. Try on your dress in its entirety—undergarments, shoes, accessories—the whole look. Walk in it. Sit in it. Dance in it (yes, really). This is your chance to catch any issues with the fit and adjust. If the lace chafes, say something! Often, the seamstress can work magic to achieve a more comfortable fit. It's also an excellent time for a mini dress rehearsal with your bridal party and practice bustling. Confidence comes from comfort, and comfort comes from preparation. Plus, slipping into your dress with no surprises on the big day? Now *that's* a good feeling.

Day 106

Vendors can give advice but trust your gut and stick to what's important.

Vendors are experts in logistics, but *you're* the expert in what matters most to you. Take their advice with gratitude, but don't feel pressured to follow every suggestion. If a song doesn't feel right, or a timeline stresses you out, speak up. Remember, they're helping *you* build your vision, not theirs. Stay true to your values, your priorities, and your relationship's vibe. You're not just putting on a show, you're telling a love story. Let the pros handle the details but let your heart guide the direction.

 Something to talk about: Do we want the first glimpse of each other in front of our guests or during a private moment?

Day 107

Remember to include tips in your wedding budget.

Don't forget to include tips in your wedding budget because those little extras can add up faster than you think. From your caterers and bartenders to the hair and makeup team who help you look your best, many of the people working behind the scenes rely on gratuities as part of their income. It's easy to focus on big-ticket items like the venue or photographer and overlook this important detail, but planning for tips ensures you can thank each vendor properly for their hard work. Do a little research ahead of time to learn what's customary and set aside labeled envelopes with cash or checks so you're not scrambling on the big day.

Beyond your vendors, consider "tipping" the people in your life who've gone above and beyond in ways money can't measure. Write a heartfelt letter to your parents, maid of honor, best man, or anyone whose love and support carried you to this moment. Tuck it away for them to read later—perhaps the morning after the wedding—so they can savor your gratitude in a quiet, personal moment. Those notes may end up being the most treasured gift you give that day.

 Conversation starter: When tipping, what are we comfortable with for standard vs. exceptional service?

Chapter 3

It's Go Time!
Keep calm and get married!

Day 108

In the end, all that matters is "I Do."

It's easy to get lost in the details such as flowers, the playlist, and place settings, but none of it matters more than those two little words. *I do* is the promise at the heart of the whole day, the reason for the celebration, not the result of it. You could have the wrong song play, the cake collapses, or the weather refuse to cooperate, and if you still stand together and make that vow, the day was a success. That's the true center of your wedding—the moment you say *"Yes"* to a lifetime together.

Keeping that perspective front and center can be a lifesaver when planning gets stressful. Fancy doesn't equal meaning. Connection does. When the to-do list feels overwhelming, take a breath and remember why you're there. It's not for perfection, it's for the promise, the love, and the future that begins with that simple, extraordinary commitment.

 Ask each other: Who are our most trustworthy people to hold our rings before and during the ceremony?

Day 109

*The wedding is one day; your marriage
will last a lifetime.*

A wedding is a big deal, but it's just the opening scene. Don't pour all your energy, money, and attention into one day and leave nothing for the days after. Marriage is the long game and the real prize. It deserves just as much planning, intention, and heart as the wedding itself. So, when you're debating whether to splurge on custom napkins or feeling crushed over a vendor hiccup, pause. Ask yourself: "Will this matter a year from now? Five years?" Keep your eyes on the forever, not just the first day.

Day 110

*Nothing is sadder than a totally plastered bride,
groom, or both.*

It's your party, and yes, you should enjoy yourself, but trust me, you'll want to remember it. A few celebratory drinks are fine, but going overboard can turn your once-in-a-lifetime day into a blurry mess, or worse, an embarrassing memory. Stay present. Feel the love, soak in the joy, and celebrate without needing to numb or escape. Have fun responsibly so you can dance, laugh, and genuinely savor every part of the day. Your future self will thank you—and so will your photographer.

 Timely Tip: A good rule is to drink water in between each cocktail.

Day 111

Steal quiet moments for just the two of you.

Weddings can feel like a marathon of hugs, photos, and conversations. But in the middle of the chaos, find each other. Step away, even for five minutes. Breathe. Look around. Say, "Can you believe this is happening?" Those quiet pauses let you ground yourself in the moment and soak it all in together. You'll remember the stolen glances, the whispered "I love you's," more than half the toasts. This day is about *you* two, so don't forget to experience it *with* each other.

Day 112

Remember to eat and stay hydrated on your wedding day.

You'd be surprised how many couples barely eat on their wedding day and end up hangry (hungry + angry) or fainting before the first dance, sometimes during the actual ceremony! Between the nerves, the photos, and the whirlwind of guests, it's easy to forget the basics. But your body needs fuel to keep up with the day's excitement. Make a plan for meals and hydration, even if it's as simple as a smoothie in a quiet room or a quick snack before the ceremony. You'll feel better, think clearly, and enjoy your reception without crashing mid-toast. You've planned so long for this day, you want to remember it!

 Conversation starter: How do you feel about leaving our wedding early if the hits us?

Day 113

Savor every moment

The day you've planned and dreamed about will fly by in what feels like minutes. It's a whirlwind of joy, hugs, music, and emotion—and if you're not careful, it can pass in a blur. So slow down. Take mental snapshots. Notice the look on your partner's face, the way your friend laughs, the feel of your hands in theirs. This is a once-in-a-lifetime moment. Don't rush through it—soak it in. Breathe deeply. Laugh fully. Let it imprint itself onto your heart. The more present you are, the more beautiful your memories will be.

Day 114

Designate a conversation wrangler and a hand signal for when you need saving.

Your wedding day will be full of warm hugs and heartfelt words, but it can also come with long-winded guests, awkward interactions, and unexpected emotional talks when you've only got 30 seconds between cake cutting and photos. Choose a trusted friend or sibling who knows your style and can politely step in when you're cornered in a never-ending chat. Maybe it's a tap on the shoulder, a gentle interruption, or swooping in with, "Sorry to interrupt, but we need you for a quick photo!" Use a subtle hand signal only your wrangler knows, like scratching your nose or adjusting your bracelet. It's a graceful escape.

 Ask each other: What does quality time mean to you?

Day 115

Set aside meals.

On your wedding day, eating often falls to the bottom of the list, but you'll need fuel to keep up with the excitement. Between greeting guests, dancing, and taking photos, it's easy to barely touch your plate. That's why it's smart to plan ahead. Ask your caterer to pack a few boxed meals with easy, handheld options like sandwiches, wraps, or sliders. Having three or four different choices means you and your new spouse can grab something quickly, even if you don't have time to sit down. It also ensures you won't be running on champagne and adrenaline alone. A little preparation goes a long way in keeping your energy up so you can truly enjoy every moment of the night.

Day 116

Pick a rendezvous spot for quiet moments.

Amid the busy joy of your wedding, don't lose sight of each other. It's easy to get swept up in guests, schedules, and traditions, but take time to reconnect. Walk hand in hand. Sit together during dinner. Sneak away for a quiet chat. These small moments create memories just for the two of you, grounding you in the reason for the day: your love, your commitment, your new beginning. The best parts of the wedding often aren't on the timeline; they're in the moments you share when you pause and just be.

 Timely Tip: Have a trusted friend stash a few bottles of water and snacks at your rendezvous spot.

Day 117

Thank your parents in a special way.

No matter how involved they were in the wedding planning, your parents have likely been part of your love story for much longer than your fiancé. Take a moment—whether it's a handwritten note, a quiet hug, or a toast—to let them know you see and appreciate their support, sacrifice, and love. Gratitude is a gift that resonates long after the day. Recognizing your parents in a meaningful way isn't just kind, it's a beautiful reminder that love grows best when it's honored across generations.

Day 118

Wear something totally ridiculous under your wedding outfit.

Think of taco socks, superhero boxers, or a hidden message on the inside hem of your dress. It's your little secret—something that reminds you not to take the day (or yourselves) *too* seriously. It's a grounding moment of fun in the middle of a high-stakes, high-heels kind of day. Plus, years later, you'll laugh remembering that under all the lace and glamour, you were secretly rocking leopard-print undies or a temporary tattoo that said, "Game On." Weddings are beautiful, but marriage is built on humor, inside jokes, and being your weird, wonderful selves. Why not start now?

 Something to talk about: What wedding traditions do you find a hard "No?"

Day 119

Trust your professionals.

You've pinned, planned, and pictured it all, but when the big day comes, hand over the reins to the pros. Your vendors have likely done hundreds of weddings; this isn't their first rodeo... or wedding! Trust their experience. Let your photographer guide the lighting, your planner handle Aunt Ruth, and your DJ read the dance floor. You hired them for a reason, so let them shine. The more you release control, the more you'll enjoy the magic. You're not just hosting an event; you're living a memory. So, relax, breathe, and let your team do what they do best.

Day 120

If you didn't drop old baggage before you walked down the aisle, drop it NOW!

We all carry a little emotional baggage but dragging it into your marriage will only weigh you both down. If there are unresolved issues from your past such as hurts, habits, or hangups, it's never too late to address them. Marriage thrives on honesty, vulnerability, and growth. What you avoid today could trip you up tomorrow. So, take a deep breath, get honest with yourself (and each other), and do the work to let go. The lighter your heart, the stronger your connection. It's better to address any issues now.

 Conversation starter: If we allow children to attend the wedding, what is the plan for when they act up?

Day 121

Don't forget to take bathroom breaks!

It sounds silly, but it's solid gold advice: don't forget to take bathroom breaks! Between the photos, the vows, the hugs, and the happy tears, it's easy to forget basic needs, like bodily functions. Plan ahead and go before you get into the dress (trust me, it's harder later), and don't be afraid to sneak away during the reception for a quick moment of relief. Don't avoid drinking water as a way to avoid the bathroom... you need both! Ask a friend to be your "bathroom buddy" if needed—it's one of those unglamorous but very real parts of the day you'll be glad you prepared for.

Day 122

No matter how much you plan, something will go wrong.

You can plan every detail, color-code your spreadsheets, and rehearse the timeline down to the minute, and still, something will go sideways. Maybe the flowers arrive late, the playlist glitches, or someone forgets the rings (it happens!) But here's the real wedding wisdom: it's not the mishaps that define the day; it's how you handle them. Roll with the punches, laugh at the chaos, and remember why you're there in the first place. Imperfections don't ruin the moment; they make the moments memorable. Some of the best stories come from things that didn't go "right."

 Ask each other: What's one thing that could go wrong on our wedding day that we could laugh about instead of stress over?

Day 123

Pick a codeword for "I need a break."

Choose a random word, like "pineapple," "jellybean," or "flamingo parade." Use it throughout the day as a secret signal when one of you needs a breather or just five minutes of silence. It's your private lifeline in the middle of the beautiful chaos. Surrounded by people, cameras, and constant motion, this silly word becomes your way of saying, "Help me sneak away." It adds a layer of inside-joke intimacy to the day, and it's also fun whispering "marshmallow" while smiling for photos and plotting your great escape to the hors d'oeuvres. Because even during the most formal moments, your weird little world together is what matters most.

Day 124

Unexpected hiccups often create the best memories.

The truth is that the moments you *don't* plan often become the ones you talk about for years. The flower girl who wandered off, the speech that went hilariously off-script, the power flicker during your first dance—those little hiccups? They're memory-makers. Perfection is overrated. It's the unexpected, slightly messy, totally human moments that give your wedding something special. When something goes sideways, smile. Take a breath. Let it be part of the story. Because long after the bouquet wilts and the cake is gone, it's those surprises that make your day uniquely, wonderfully yours. Embrace the beauty of imperfection.

 Conversation starter: What's a time in the past when something went off track but still turned out to be a great memory?

Day 125

When things go wrong, just remember why you're here.

When something goes off-script, pause and remind yourself why you're here. Not for the perfect photos, the centerpieces, or the "chicken or steak" debate. You're here because you found your person. The one you laugh with, cry with, and will build a life with. The rest is background noise. When you keep your heart focused on love, not logistics, everything that truly matters remains. So, if it rains, if the cake leans, or if someone shows up in white who definitely shouldn't, let it go. Take your partner's hand, take a breath, and soak in the moment you'll both remember forever.

Day 126

If you have a fluffy dress, assign at least two bridesmaids as official bathroom helpers.

If your dress is fluffy, layered, or princess-level poofy, you're going to need a bathroom support team. Assign at least two bridesmaids as your official bathroom helpers (bonus points if they're patient and have strong arms). Maneuvering tulle, buttons, and a train in a tiny stall is not a solo sport. They'll hold, fluff, zip, and offer emotional support while you navigate the logistics of simply... sitting. It's awkward, hilarious, and totally necessary.

 Timely Tip: Create a Messy Moment Mantra to repeat when things go wrong, such as "This will be a great story later," or "We're here for the love."

Day 127

Eat little and often throughout the day.

With nerves fluttering and things moving fast, food can easily become an afterthought, but trust me, you'll need the fuel. A well-fed bride or groom is a happy one, so plan for easy, protein-rich snacks. Delegate someone to hand you a sandwich or snack between the ceremony and photos. And yes, sit down and enjoy your reception meal, even if it's just a few quiet bites together at the sweetheart table. Hunger can tank your energy and mood; don't let it steal your joy. Eating is self-care, and self-care makes everything feel better.

Day 128

Everyone gets the post-wedding blues.

After the whirlwind of planning, attention, and celebration, it's normal to feel a little deflated. Post-wedding blues are real, and they don't mean anything is wrong. You've just spent months or years building up to one magical day, and now it's over. That shift can be jarring. Instead of panicking, allow yourself space to come down gently. Focus on building the next chapter together. Create new routines, make new memories, and keep the joy going in a different form. Your wedding was one beautiful day. Your marriage is the adventure that follows.

 Conversation starter: What is one thing you will miss once we're married?

The best wedding day memories are usually the unplanned ones.

Chapter 4

Becoming a "We" Without Losing the "Me"

Day 129

Don't keep score.

Keeping score in a relationship turns love into a competition that no one wins. It's tempting to mentally tally who took out the trash last, who planned more date nights, or who apologized first. However, that mindset fosters resentment rather than trust. Relationships aren't about even splits; they're about shared effort, not perfect symmetry. The moment you start measuring love in points, you lose sight of the bigger picture: you're on the same team.

There will be seasons when one of you is giving more emotionally, financially, and/or physically. That's okay. What matters is the willingness to step up when your partner can't, and to trust that they'll do the same for you. Love thrives when it's given freely, not conditionally. A strong relationship isn't 50/50, it's two people showing up with their whole hearts, even when their capacity looks different. If you're constantly counting, you're not connecting. And when you stop counting, you'll start noticing the love already around you.

 Ask each other: Time with friends is important, but how much time is too much?

Day 130

Don't let family interfere.

Family can be loving, supportive, and sometimes a little too involved. Boundaries are essential for protecting your relationship from outside pressure. Everyone has opinions, but at the end of the day, your marriage is between *you two*. Respect your families, but don't let them steer the ship. Communicate as a couple first and present a united front. Learning to lovingly say "this is our decision" sets the tone for a relationship rooted in mutual respect and independence. Honor your roots but prioritize your new foundation.

Day 131

Treat each other with as much respect as you would a stranger.

It's funny how we often show more patience with a stranger than with the person we love most. In the heat of frustration, it's easy to forget basic courtesy, but respect is the oxygen of love. Treat your partner with the same kindness, tone, and dignity you'd offer a friend or acquaintance. Say "please" and "thank you." Listen when they speak. Respect doesn't mean agreeing all the time; it means disagreeing with kindness and consideration. When you lead with respect, even in challenging moments, you build a relationship where love and safety go hand in hand.

 Conversation starter: What do you like best about each other's family?

Day 132

Start your own traditions.

While family customs and social media highlight reels offer inspiration, your relationship deserves its own signature style. Maybe it's a Sunday morning walk uptown for breakfast at your special brunch spot, handwritten anniversary letters, or a yearly trip to the beach. Traditions are anchors; they give your relationship rhythm, comfort, and shared meaning. You don't need a reason to start one. Over time, those little rituals become some of your favorite memories. Creating traditions together isn't just fun, it's a way of saying, "This is who we are, and how we love."

Day 133

Be prepared to work hard!

Marriage isn't always a walk in the park; it's often more like hiking uphill in the rain, holding hands the whole way. It requires effort, patience, compromise, and constant tending. Love alone isn't enough; it takes intentional action, especially during hard seasons. However, the reward is immense: growth, deep connection, and a sense of partnership that can weather any challenge. Don't fear hard work, embrace it. When both people commit to building something strong, the result is a life filled with meaning, even when the path is messy.

 Something to talk about: Do you view vacations as a necessity or a luxury?

Day 134

*Every day, ask your partner what was the best
and worst part of their day.*

This simple question opens the door to daily connection. It's an invitation to share joy, process stress, and feel seen. When you check in with your partner like this, you're saying, "I care about your world." It builds emotional intimacy and reminds you to stay engaged with each other's lives beyond chores and logistics. You don't need long, deep conversations every night, just consistent moments of intentional listening. Little daily questions can lead to big understanding and closeness.

Day 135

A healthy sex life is an important part of a happy marriage.

Physical intimacy is more than just a moment; it's a powerful connector. A thriving sex life often reflects good communication, emotional safety, and mutual care. It's not about frequency or performance; it's about prioritizing closeness, pleasure, and vulnerability. Talk openly about what you need and enjoy. Make time for it, even when life gets busy. When you protect that space, you nourish your bond in a way that words alone can't always do. A healthy sex life isn't everything, but it *is* something worth protecting.

 Finish this sentence: I think a healthy sex life is...

Day 136

A marriage is between two people—hard stop!

Everyone will have opinions, but only two people are in the marriage. That means you and your partner get to decide what works for *you*, even if it looks different than what others expect. Don't let outside voices drown out your inner compass. Boundaries are key, and so is communication. This includes parents and even close friends who have your best interests at heart. When decisions are made together as a married couple, with honesty and unity, they're stronger. You can listen to advice from others, but don't let them write your story.

Day 137

A relationship can't thrive by each partner giving 50%.

The idea of "meeting halfway" sounds fair, but it can lead to keeping score or holding back. Healthy relationships aren't about splitting everything evenly; they're about showing up fully. Give 100%, even when it's hard, but know that your 100% today might not look like yesterday's. Some days your all-in effort is big; other days, it's simply being kind through exhaustion. And that's okay. What matters is giving the best of what you *have* in that moment. Love thrives not on perfect math, but on mutual care and daily effort. Show up with heart, grace, and the willingness to keep choosing each other.

 Ask each other: What are your views on the roles of each partner?

Day 138

"Accept the things to which fate binds you and love the people with whom fate brings you together but do so with all your heart."— Marcus Aurelius

Life is unpredictable. People cross your path unexpectedly. Love often arrives without warning. Accepting what fate brings doesn't mean being passive; it means embracing the present fully. When you meet someone worth loving, don't hold back. Love them with intention and kindness. Not because they're perfect, but because life is short, and love is rare. Cherish the connection fate offered you. Commit to it, water it and let it grow.

Day 139

All weddings are similar, but every marriage is unique.

All weddings have a familiar rhythm—vows, rings, cake, and dancing—but every marriage is one-of-a-kind. Don't be fooled by picture-perfect moments; what comes after is where the fundamental differences truly reveal themselves. Your marriage will be shaped by your quirks, your values, and how you two choose to navigate life together. Some couples thrive on routines, others on spontaneity. Some talk everything out; others need space first. There's no single "right" way to do marriage. While your wedding might look like others on the surface, permit yourselves to build a marriage that looks like *you.*

 Conversation starter: As a couple, what do we want out of life?

Day 140

Always make sure your spouse is a priority.

Life gets full of work, kids, friends, and to-dos, but your spouse should remain at the top of your priority list, right there next to yourself. That doesn't mean ignoring everything else; it means making sure they never feel like they're coming in last. Check in. Plan time together. Be intentional about staying emotionally close. When your partner knows they're your person, they feel safe, seen, and valued. That kind of love feeds the relationship in all the right ways. Put each other first, and everything else will feel more manageable.

Day 141

Always respond affectionately to affection.

When your partner reaches for you, whether with a touch, a kind word, or an emotional moment, respond with warmth. Affection doesn't always have to lead to sex, and it doesn't require a big display. But it *does* deserve a response. A squeeze of the hand, a soft smile, a "thanks, I needed that" are small gestures that say, *I see you, I feel you, I'm here.* Brushing off affection, even unintentionally, can slowly create distance. Over time, those missed moments can feel like rejection. So even if you're tired, distracted, or not in the mood for more, respond with tenderness. It's not about giving everything; it's about giving *something*.

 Ask each other: What is something I do that makes you smile?

Day 142

Avoid debt whenever possible.

Debt can quietly creep in and become a major source of stress in a marriage. While some debt (like a home or education) can be strategic, borrowing for things that quickly lose value, like clothes, vacations, or a lavish party, can put pressure on your future. Living within your means isn't about deprivation; it's about freedom. The fewer financial burdens you carry, the more peace, flexibility, and options you have. Make decisions that honor both your present joy and your future goals. Spend wisely so you can build a life that's rich in what matters.

Day 143

Keep doing the thoughtful things you did for each other while dating.

Kindness is love's most powerful habit. The small, thoughtful things like notes, hugs, compliments, and surprises, shouldn't stop after the vows. If anything, they matter more. It's easy to fall into routine, but consistent kindness keeps the spark alive. Treat each other with the same curiosity, excitement, and attentiveness you did when you first fell in love. Keep dating each other. Keep noticing. Keep appreciating. Long-lasting love isn't built on big gestures, it's built on a thousand tiny moments of choosing to care for, to notice, and to show up with tenderness.

 Conversation starter: How do you feel about credit card and personal loan debt?

Day 144

Marriage must evolve to survive.

Stagnant love doesn't grow. Life changes and a healthy marriage adapts. That means listening, learning, adjusting, and sometimes letting go of your way to make space for something better. Compromise isn't a loss; it's a gift you give your relationship. New ideas, routines, and roles are opportunities to evolve together. The more flexible you are, the stronger your bond becomes. Rigidity leads to distance. Openness leads to discovery, and discovery keeps love alive.

Day 145

Be truly interested in learning more about your partner.

Just because you're married doesn't mean you know *everything* about your partner. People grow, shift, and surprise—even the ones you share a bathroom with. Stay curious and ask questions. Pay attention to what lights them up or weighs them down. Continue exploring each other like you're still dating. Lifelong interest builds intimacy. When you continue to learn about your partner, you deepen and think more thoughtfully about your love for them. Don't assume, ask questions. Don't settle into autopilot, stay engaged. They're worth it and so is your connection.

 Something to talk about: How do you think our relationship will change after we're married?

Day 146

Build a nest egg and agree on how you'll use it.

Money can be a source of security or a source of stress, and a lot of that depends on how intentionally you manage it. Start saving early, even if it's just a little at a time. More importantly, talk openly about what that money is *for*. Emergencies? A house? A dream trip? Shared goals give your savings purpose and keep you aligned as a team. Avoid secret accounts or unspoken assumptions. Your financial health isn't just about numbers, it's about trust, planning, and dreaming together for the life you're building.

Day 147

Buy earplugs.

Seriously, buy earplugs. Whether it's snoring, early alarms, or late-night TV, protecting your sleep can protect your patience. You'll love each other more when you're both well-rested. While we don't suggest having a TV in the bedroom, earplugs can help you find peace if your spouse insists on one. This isn't about avoiding connection; it's about finding practical ways to live peacefully together. Little annoyances don't have to turn into big frustrations. Sometimes, love means adapting with a sense of humor and a bit of foam in your ears. It's one of the smallest purchases that can make a surprisingly big difference.

 Conversation starter: If snoring becomes an issue, how do you feel about separate bedrooms?

Day 148

*Carve your initials and wedding date on the
tree in the backyard.*

Symbolic gestures, such as carving your initials, are sweet reminders of your commitment. It's not about the tree; it's about marking your love on something rooted and growing. Traditions like this create emotional touchstones—little places in your shared life where you can say, "We started here." Whether it's a tree, a photo, or a handwritten note tucked into a drawer, find a way to anchor your beginning in something you can return to again and again. Let your love leave a visible mark in the world.

Day 149

Constantly turn toward each other.

Constantly turning toward each other is one of the quiet habits that keeps love alive. It's about small moments, such as looking up when they walk in the room, reaching for their hand, listening when they speak instead of scrolling your phone. These little choices send a powerful message: *you matter, I see you, I'm here.* Marriage isn't built on grand gestures nearly as much as it is on everyday signals of care and connection. When stress pulls you in opposite directions, those tiny pivots back toward each other keep you anchored. Keep choosing closeness over distance, attention over distraction, and love over indifference. Over time, those small turns create a marriage that feels safe, steady, and deeply connected.

 Ask each other: What is the one thing you worry most about?

Day 150

Create partnership rituals.

Partnership rituals are the glue that quietly holds a relationship together. They don't have to be big or complicated; sometimes it's as simple as a morning coffee together, a Sunday night walk, or a kiss before leaving the house. These rituals become touchstones in the rhythm of your life, reminders that no matter how busy or chaotic things get, you always come back to each other. They anchor you in routine while keeping love intentional. Over time, these small traditions build a sense of safety, joy, and belonging. A strong marriage isn't just built on milestones, it's nurtured in the everyday moments you choose to repeat, protect, and cherish together.

Day 151

Rely on your spouse, not your parents.

Your family may love you deeply, but your primary emotional support should now be your spouse. That shift can be challenging, especially if you're close with your parents, but it's essential for building a healthy marriage. Turning towards your partner first promotes trust, intimacy, and teamwork. It says, "We're in this together." Your parents can still play a role, but your spouse is your person now. Create space to grow independently as a couple, and your bond will deepen in powerful ways.

 Conversation Starter: What do you rely on your parents for that we should handle as a married couple?

Day 152

View chores as a gift to your spouse.

Chores aren't just tasks; they're acts of love. When you wash the dishes, take out the trash, or fold the laundry, you're saying, "I care about our life together." Instead of resenting the responsibilities, reframe them. What if cleaning the bathroom or running an errand was less about duty and more about kindness? When both people contribute with a spirit of generosity, the home becomes a place of peace and partnership, not pressure. Love lives in the little things, including wiping down the counters.

Day 153

Don't boss each other around.

Marriage should feel like a partnership, not a tug-of-war. You can get things done by being bossy, but at the cost of connection and respect. Requests are more powerful than commands, and how you say something often matters more than what you say. Timing counts, too. Speak with kindness, even when you're frustrated. Your partner isn't your assistant or your to-do list manager; they're your teammate. Talk to them in a way that invites unity, not control. The words you choose and the tone you use both shape the emotional climate of your relationship. Build one rooted in grace, patience, and mutual dignity. You're not managing each other; you're building a life together.

 Something to talk about: How do you feel about hired help? (cleaning, lawn maintenance, etc.)

Day 154

Don't have kids because others are pressuring you.

Having children is a beautiful, life-changing decision that should come from a deep, mutual desire, not pressure from family, friends, or ticking clocks. Everyone will have opinions, but only the two of you will be doing the daily work of raising, loving, and shaping that child's world. Don't rush it. Please don't do it to check a box or quiet the questions. Make room for honest conversations about timing, fears, finances, and the kind of life you want to build. Readiness isn't about perfection; it's about alignment. It's about being on the same page and being willing to grow together, even when it's hard. This is your life, your family, and your future. Let it unfold on *your* terms.

Day 155

Don't smother each other.

A strong relationship doesn't require being attached to the hip. While quality time together is essential, so is maintaining your own identity. Hobbies, friends, and quiet spaces aren't threats, they're fuel. Time apart helps you reconnect with more to share, more to give, and more to appreciate in one another. Smothering creates pressure, not closeness. Give each other room to breathe, grow, and to just *be*. The healthiest couples are the ones who can stand strong on their own and choose each other again, day after day.

 Ask each other: How long do you think we should wait to have kids?

Day 156

Plan a few vacations for just the two of you.

Plan a few vacations for just the two of you, especially early on. It's easy to get swept into family trips, group getaways, or holidays with in-laws, but carving out time to travel as a couple is essential. This is your chance to start your own traditions, explore the world together, and build memories that are yours alone. Whether it's a weekend road trip or a big international adventure, traveling without the buffer of extended family helps you learn how you move through the world as a team. The family vacations will still be there, but these couple-only getaways lay the groundwork for a stronger bond, deeper connection, and a lifetime of inside jokes. Start now and travel together before life gets louder.

Day 157

Don't lose yourself after you become a spouse.

Love is about connection, not fusion. Sure, you're now a bonded couple, but you're still you. Keep your passions, friendships, and independence alive. A strong marriage is built on two whole people choosing to grow together, not on one person disappearing into the other. When you stay grounded in who you are, you bring more energy, perspective, and joy into the relationship. Don't trade your individuality for intimacy; real connection happens when both of you show up fully, as yourselves.

 Something to talk about: What is one thing you did as a single person that you want to continue to do in marriage?

Day 158

Draw the line with in-laws before they become outlaws.

Healthy in-law relationships are built on mutual respect and clear boundaries. If expectations aren't addressed early, tensions can build, and loyalty can be tested. Talk as a couple about what feels comfortable and present a united front when setting limits. Boundaries aren't about shutting people out; they're about protecting your marriage. Whether it's input on holidays, parenting, or how often they drop by, clear communication keeps things from spiraling. It's easier to set boundaries now than untangle drama later.

Day 159

Falling in love is the easy part; staying in love takes work.

Falling in love is effortless, full of chemistry, late-night talks, and butterflies. But staying in love? That's where the real magic (and effort) begins. It means choosing each other on the hard days, showing up with kindness when you're tired, and continuing to nurture the bond long after the honeymoon phase fades. Just as a fire won't burn without fuel, love needs tending It's built on the little things: listening without distraction, apologizing sincerely, laughing often, and growing together through life's changes. Staying in love isn't about perfection; it's about presence.

 Conversation starter: What values do each of us want to bring into our marriage?

Day 160

Give the gift of your time by doing something for your spouse that they don't like to do.

It might not be glamorous, but taking over a dreaded chore, such as cleaning the bathroom, scheduling the dentist appointments, or folding laundry can be a powerful act of love. It says, "I see what drains you, and I've got you." These small, selfless gestures speak volumes. They show your partner that their comfort matters more than your convenience. Love isn't just candlelit dinners, it's also taking out the trash, so they don't have to. Give your time and energy. It's the thoughtfulness behind the task that makes it unforgettable.

Day 161

Don't stop opening doors.

Chivalry shouldn't end when the honeymoon begins. Simple gestures like opening a door or pulling out a chair aren't about old-fashioned roles; they're about intentional kindness. They say, "I still want to make you feel cared for." Romance doesn't have to be grand to be meaningful. It's often in the little, everyday choices that love is kept alive. Keep doing small things. Keep showing up in the ways that make your partner feel seen and appreciated. Those tiny acts, repeated over time, become the threads that weave lasting love. And when life gets hectic, those gestures serve as gentle reminders that your relationship is still a priority.

 Ask each other: What is the thing you like most about yourself?

Day 162

Guys, don't lose touch with your friends.

Time with your partner is essential, but time with your friends is also important. Especially male friendships, which offer a unique kind of support, perspective, and play that no romantic relationship can fully replace. Grabbing a drink, hitting the golf course, or just venting with a buddy helps you reset and recharge. It's not "time away from your relationship," it's part of staying emotionally healthy *within* it. Your spouse doesn't need to be your everything. Let friendship be part of your balance.

Day 163

If you and your spouse don't share the same hobbies, find friends who do.

You don't have to like all the same things to love each other. It's okay if one of you loves hiking while the other prefers movies. Instead of forcing it, honor it. Enjoy your shared interests together and let friends fill the gap in other areas. This gives each of you space to thrive individually, which only strengthens the relationship. You'll return to each other refreshed, with stories to share, and maybe a little more appreciation for your differences. And who knows—every once in a while, you might even surprise each other by joining in and discovering a new shared joy.

 Conversation starter: How should we choose our first (or next) pet?

Day 164

If you both focus on meeting each other's needs first, you'll create a better relationship than you ever imagined.

Selflessness is powerful in marriage—*when it's mutual.* When both partners are attuned to each other's needs, you create a cycle of giving that fosters deep trust and joy. It's not about neglecting yourself, it's about leaning in with love and saying, "I'm here for you." When each person puts the other first, everyone wins. Needs get met, love multiplies, and the relationship becomes a safe, generous space that neither of you wants to leave.

Day 165

---

*If you're having a bad day, say so... this way
your partner knows what to expect.*

You don't have to pretend everything's fine all the time. Being honest about your emotional state isn't a burden; it's a gift. It helps your partner understand you, support you, and avoid misreading your mood. Instead of snapping or withdrawing, try saying, "I'm having a rough one today." It sets expectations and invites connection instead of confusion. Communication doesn't have to be deep to be effective; it just needs to be honest. Being real about your bad days strengthens trust and keeps resentment at bay. It also reassures your partner that they can do the same, creating space for both of you to be fully human.

 Something to talk about: How do you like to spend your days off?

Day 166

Keep family and friends out of your decision-making.

Advice is easy to come by, but your relationship doesn't need a committee. While support is wonderful, your most important decisions should stay between you and your partner. Too many outside opinions can cloud your judgment and create unnecessary pressure. Talk things through privately. Trust your instincts as a couple. It's your life, your marriage, and your choices. Outside noise fades when the two of you are aligned, and that's where peace lives. The strongest couples aren't the ones who follow the loudest voices, but the ones who learn to stand together, confident in their own path.

Day 167

Ladies, mark your monthly cycle on the calendar.

Marking your monthly cycle on the calendar isn't just for yourself, but for the health of your relationship. Knowing when your period is coming helps you understand your mood shifts, energy levels, and even how you communicate. You're not being "too sensitive," you're being affected by real hormonal changes, and that awareness is power. It can help you give yourself more grace, plan around your needs, and even let your partner in on what's going on emotionally or physically. This gives your partner a chance to support you thoughtfully, not accidentally step on landmines.

 Conversation starter: If we come to an impasse with a decision, how do we approach the tiebreaker?

Day 168

Ladies: Don't lose touch with your girlfriends.

Your partner may be your main person, but your girlfriends are vital too. They offer perspective, laughter, and support you don't always get from your spouse. That's not a flaw in your marriage; it's a strength in your life. When you nurture your friendships, you maintain your identity and emotional health, which benefits your relationship. Don't put your social circle on pause once you say, "I do." There will be days when your girlfriends help you breathe, laugh, and remind you of who you are. Keep them close. They're part of your happily ever after, too.

Day 169

Meet your spouse's needs today by choosing a gesture that says, "I cherish you."

Love isn't just something you say, it's something you show. And it doesn't have to be grand. A small gesture, like their favorite coffee waiting in the car, a quick shoulder rub, or a handwritten note, speaks volumes. Every day presents a new opportunity to show your partner that they matter. Instead of waiting for a special occasion, ask yourself, "What can I do today that says, 'I cherish you'?" It's these daily acts of care that keep love alive. Over time, those little gestures create a foundation of warmth and security that no single grand gesture could ever replace.

 Conversation starter: How do you feel about putting kids into childcare?

Day 170

Don't completely tie your finances together.

While shared finances are a smart and practical part of marriage, having a little money that's just yours can be a quiet game-changer. It's not about hiding things, it's about keeping a sense of self. A personal fund gives you the guiltless freedom to treat yourself, pursue hobbies, or buy that quirky thing your partner just doesn't understand . It helps money remain as a tool, not a source of tension or control. The key is open communication: discuss your financial setup, agree on what feels fair, and revisit it as life changes. Marriage is about building together, but keeping a little corner of financial independence can bring a lot of peace, self-trust, and mutual respect along the way.

Day 171

Never cut your toenails in bed.

Some rules are less about romance and more about respect, and this is one of them: never clip your nails in bed. Nothing kills the mood faster than stray clippings hiding in the sheets. Marriage is about loving each other through quirks, but there's a line between charming and downright gross. Keep grooming where it belongs— in the bathroom, not in the place meant for rest and intimacy. It's not about being fussy; it's about being thoughtful. Protecting your shared space with small, considerate choices shows you value your partner's comfort just as much as your own.

 Ask each other: How do you feel about each having some separate finances?

Day 172

Don't wallpaper with your spouse.

Consider this a metaphor and practical guidance. Some activities, especially those requiring patience, precision, and glue, can test the best of marriages. Avoid unnecessary stress by knowing which tasks are better suited for solo work or professional assistance. In marriage, teamwork is essential but so is knowing your limits as a duo. Not every project needs to be a bonding moment. Choose your time together wisely and know when to delegate. The wallpaper will look better, and your relationship will feel better, too.

Day 173

No man has ever been shot doing dishes.

There's truth in the humor when saying no man has ever been shot doing dishes. Sharing chores isn't just about dividing the workload, it's about showing respect, teamwork, and love in action. When one partner takes on the small, everyday tasks, it lifts a weight off the other and says, *"I see you. I've got you."* A clean kitchen might not sound romantic but trust me, acts of service like this often mean more than flowers or fancy dinners. Marriage thrives when both partners pitch in, no matter how unglamorous the job is. Roll up your sleeves, grab the sponge, and remember suds and smiles can go hand in hand.

 Conversation starter: How should we divide household duties?

Day 174

Commit to making your bedroom a sanctuary.

Commit to making your bedroom a sanctuary—a calm, screen-free space where connection comes first. No cell phones, no TV, no hygiene routines in bed. This isn't about being anti-technology, it's about being *pro-intimacy*. Your bedroom should be a retreat, not a second living room or a mobile office. When you leave the distractions at the door, you make room for conversation, cuddling, quiet, and real rest. Even ten minutes of undistracted time together at the end of the day can strengthen your bond more than hours of background noise ever could. Protect that space. Let it be a place where the world fades and only the two of you remain.

Day 175

Nothing can hurt your marriage more than unrealistic expectations.

Fairy tales are lovely, but real love lives in the everyday. Expecting your spouse to fulfill every need, never annoy you, or read your mind is a setup for disappointment. Unrealistic expectations are like invisible tripwires where, eventually, someone stumbles. Choose grace over perfection and growth over fantasy. Marriage isn't always about getting it right; it's about working through the mess, learning together, and choosing each other anyway. Love blooms best when it's rooted in reality.

 Something to talk about: What have you always wanted to do, but were too scared to attempt?

Day 176

Once the wedding is over, don't stop planning.

Your wedding is just the starting line. So keep dreaming and planning! Whether it's a weekend trip, a five-year goal, or retirement dreams, having things to look forward to keeps your relationship energized. It helps you stay aligned as a team and create shared excitement beyond the day-to-day. When you plan together, you grow together. Life is full of next steps, both big and small. Celebrate each one, and keep reaching for new adventures, together. The journey feels richer when you always have something on the horizon to anticipate side by side.

Day 177

Recognize that your spouse is integral to, not responsible for, your future success.

Behind every fulfilled, thriving person is often a partner who believes in them. Your spouse is more than a companion; they're your ally, sounding board, and cheerleader. Include them in your dreams. Value their input. Celebrate their support. When you rise, they rise with you. Your success isn't just personal, it's shared. Building a life together means recognizing the influence, encouragement, and strength you give one another. Don't take it for granted. Acknowledge it, often.

 Conversation starter: How would you like to spend your favorite holidays?

Day 178

Create a budget that you both can live with.

A strong financial plan reflects shared values. It's not just about bills, savings and investing; it's about living with purpose and generosity. Talk about your priorities. Set goals. Build a budget that covers the essentials *and* leaves room for joy. Don't forget to give back because charity strengthens your values and connection. And don't skimp on the "fun" fund. Enjoying your money together is just as important as managing it wisely. A budget should feel like a roadmap, not a cage.

Day 179

Share everything: covers, dreams, and the last bit of ice cream.

Marriage is built on sharing everything, both big things and the little ones. It's not just about splitting a mortgage or a bank account, but about letting each other into every corner of life. Share the covers on a cold night, your dreams for the future, and even that last spoonful of ice cream. These small gestures say, "what's mine is yours, and what's yours is ours." They build trust, intimacy, and the sense that you're always on the same team. Sharing isn't about losing, it's about multiplying joy, comfort, and connection by letting your partner in. That's how love grows, one scoop (or dream) at a time.

 Ask each other: How do you feel about charitable donations? Which cause(s) do you feel strongly about?

Day 180

Stop acting like you're single.

Marriage means your choices no longer affect just you; they ripple through the life you're building together. Staying out until 2 a.m. without checking in, making big purchases on impulse, or keeping secrets might have worked when you were single, but in marriage it creates cracks. Partnership is about respect and consideration, not control. Checking in isn't about asking permission, it's about showing you care enough to keep your spouse in the loop. When you shift from "me" to "we," you strengthen trust, build security, and create a foundation where both of you feel valued. Love thrives when you act like teammates, not roommates.

Day 181

The best way to make your spouse more loving is to be extra loving to them.

With love, what you give has a way of coming back. When you lead with gentleness, affection, and generosity, your partner often responds kindly, not out of obligation, but because it feels good to be met with love. Instead of keeping a tally of what you're not receiving, ask yourself what energy you're bringing in. Are you setting a tone of kindness or tension? Love is most impactful when it's intentional, not reactive. It's not about being a doormat, it's about being a spark. Make compassion your reflex, even on the hard days. The beauty of love is that it often grows in the space you create for it.

 Something to talk about: What is the thing you most admire about each other?

Day 182

*The more you invest in a relationship, the
more valuable it becomes.*

The more you invest in a relationship, the more valuable it becomes, not because you're keeping score, but because love deepens with intentional effort. Time, attention, and thoughtfulness are the deposits that grow trust and connection. Just like a savings account, small, steady investments add up. Check in. Show up. Say thank you. Celebrate wins, big or small. When you consistently pour into your relationship, you create something rich and lasting. It's not about grand gestures or constant perfection; it's about building a foundation of care that gets stronger over time. Love isn't found fully formed; it's built.

Day 183

The shorter the leash, the further they'll stray.

Control might feel like protection, but in reality, it pushes people away. Trust is the foundation of lasting love, not surveillance or constant check-ins. When someone feels smothered, they start craving space, and that space can quickly turn into distance. Healthy relationships are built on freedom, not fear. Give your partner room to breathe, grow, and be themselves. Trust them enough to let go a little. Ironically, the more secure someone feels in your trust, the less they feel the need to test it. Love thrives in open spaces, not tight grips.

 Conversation starter: What three things do you want to be remembered for?

Day 184

There is no such thing as man's work or woman's work.

Laundry doesn't care about gender and neither does cooking, budgeting, yard work, or plunging a clogged toilet. Marriage is a partnership, not a performance of outdated roles. The goal isn't to split everything perfectly down the middle, but to support each other where it counts. If one of you hates doing dishes and the other doesn't mind, great! Trade that task for something else. Fairness doesn't mean sameness; it means respect. Toss the scorecard and build a rhythm that works for both of you. When each person pitches in, steps up, and stays flexible, you create a home where teamwork thrives, and no one feels like they're carrying the load alone.

Day 185

Today is special... wear the fancy lingerie.

Don't wait for anniversaries to add a little spark. Romance thrives on surprise, spontaneity, and intention. Wearing the "fancy" stuff just because can be a playful reminder that attraction doesn't fade with time, it just needs a nudge now and then. Feeling good in your skin (and silk) isn't about perfection, it's about confidence and fun. So, dust off the lace, strike a pose, and enjoy the extra smile you'll put on your partner's face (and maybe your own!).

 Ask each other: How will we protect our marriage against stagnation?

Day 186

Try to outdo each other with kindness.

Try to outdo each other with kindness, not in a competitive way, but in a "let me love you even better" kind of way. Bring them coffee before they ask. Leave a note on the mirror. Brag about them in public. Kindness in marriage isn't about grand gestures; it's about the tiny, consistent choices that say, "You matter to me." When both of you are looking for ways to lift each other up instead of keeping score or waiting to be appreciated first, love becomes the default. Challenges feel lighter, and joy shows up in the ordinary. It's a cycle worth feeding, so give more, care more, and notice more. Kindness is a daily decision to lead with love.

Day 187

Try to have separate bathrooms.

Separate bathrooms might sound like a luxury, but for many couples, it's a secret to long-term harmony. It's not about avoiding each other, it's about preserving a little space for peace, privacy, and personal quirks. One partner might leave toothpaste caps off, while the other likes spotless counters. Separate bathrooms mean fewer petty arguments over clutter, more room for personal routines, and a touch of independence within your shared life. Of course, not every home makes this possible, but the bigger point is finding ways to honor each other's comfort zones. Sometimes, a little space really is what keeps love flowing.

 Conversation starter: What legal documents need to be updated?

Day 188

Verbally praise your spouse for something they've done out of love for someone.

Affirmation isn't just nice, it's necessary. When your partner goes out of their way to help, show up, or support someone else, say something. Let them know you noticed. Praise reinforces connection and values. Whether it's helping a friend move, comforting a neighbor, or volunteering at school, your words of recognition feed their soul. Public or private, a "That was really kind of you" goes a long way. Your partner isn't just your teammate; they're a human doing beautiful things. Celebrate that!

Day 189

Volunteer together.

Doing good as a team does *you* good, too. Volunteering is a great way to build shared values, gain perspective, and strengthen your bond beyond the walls of your home. Whether it's serving meals, mentoring youth, or cleaning up your community, giving back brings you closer together. It reminds you both that love extends outward and that you're part of something bigger. It's easy to get caught up in your own world, and volunteering helps you stay grounded, connected, and grateful. Plus, there's nothing more attractive than seeing your partner light up while helping others.

 Something to talk about: How can we ensure we spend quality time together?

Day 190

When you get frustrated, don't take it out on your spouse.

We all have bad days. But your partner should be your safe place, not your punching bag. When you're frustrated, pause. Breathe. Speak from emotion, not explosion. It's okay to vent, but it's not okay to unload anger like a dump truck. Learning to express frustration constructively is one of the most significant gifts you can give your relationship. It keeps conflict clean, communication honest, and resentment off the table. You're a team, so treat each other like allies, not targets.

Day 191

A sacrifice isn't for your partner; it's for your relationship.

When you give something up or compromise, it's not about losing; it's about choosing what matters most: *us.* Healthy relationships require give and take, and sometimes that means setting aside your preferences, time, or comfort for the sake of the connection. It's not about keeping score or being the "bigger person." It's about investing in the life you're building together. A true sacrifice is a gift to the relationship itself; it's a sign that you're willing to protect, nurture, and prioritize the bond, instead of being right or getting your way. When both partners do this with love and mutual respect, it strengthens the foundation and reminds you that you're in this together.

 Finish this sentence: When someone is angry with me...

Day 192

---

*When you want your spouse to do something, ask
nicely, then appreciate their effort.*

Communication works best when it's clear, kind, and followed by gratitude. Hints, sighs, or silent stares rarely get the job done. Say what you need in a specific, respectful way. Then, when your partner follows through, thank them, even if the towels are folded "wrong", the dishes aren't perfect, or the dinner is not as spicy as you like it. Appreciation builds motivation. Criticism builds walls. Celebrate the effort, not just the outcome, and watch your partnership thrive on mutual respect instead of silent expectations.

Day 193

---

*When your spouse asks for a favor, consider saying
'I'd love to' (without sarcasm!)*

When your spouse asks for a favor, try responding with, "I'd love to"—and mean it. It's a small shift in language that turns a task into an act of love. Instead of sighing, rolling your eyes, or making it feel like a burden, saying "I'd love to" communicates willingness, care, and partnership. Even when it's something small like grabbing a glass of water, running an errand, or helping with chores, it reminds your partner that you're on their side. Tone matters here, too; avoid sarcasm and let your words carry genuine warmth. Over time, these little moments of kindness build an atmosphere where both of you feel valued, supported, and cherished.

 Finish this sentence: When I feel taken advantage of, I...

Day 194

Build a satisfying relationship with your in-laws.

You're not just marrying a person; you're joining a family. While every in-law dynamic is different, making a genuine effort goes a long way. Find common ground, offer kindness, and look for ways to connect. You don't have to be best friends, but building trust and respect helps your spouse feel supported and keeps family dynamics from becoming stressful. Relationships with in-laws can be tricky, but with patience and boundaries, they can also be a surprising source of strength. And when you approach those relationships with grace, you show your partner that you value not only them but the people who helped shape them.

Day 195

Work to have the best marriage of everyone you know.

When you work to have the best marriage of everyone you know, you're not looking to impress others; you're working to inspire yourselves. Be the couple that laughs often, listens well, and holds hands long after the honeymoon phase. Celebrate each other loudly, support each other quietly, and never stop learning how to love better. A strong marriage doesn't just happen; it's built, day by day and choice by choice. Let your relationship be a safe place, the soft place, and the fun place. Compete only with yesterday's version of yourselves. Strive for a partnership that feels rare, intentional, and deeply connected.

 Ask each other: Do either of our families have apprehensions about our marriage? Why?

Day 196

Write unexpected love notes.

Write unexpected love notes—not just on birthdays or anniversaries, but on ordinary Tuesdays, in lunch bags, on bathroom mirrors, or tucked into coat pockets. A few heartfelt funny, flirty, or deeply sincere words can turn someone's whole day around. Love notes don't have to be long or poetic; they just have to be *true*. "I'm proud of you." "You make life better." "Can't wait to kiss your face later." These little surprises remind your partner that they're seen, appreciated, and adored even in the middle of daily chaos. Over time, those notes become small love landmarks, which become evidence that you didn't just say, "I do," but that you keep saying, "I still do."

Day 197

You can't change your spouse.

Trying to change your partner is a fast track to frustration. Real love isn't about improvement projects; it's about acceptance. Growth comes naturally when people feel safe, supported, and loved for who they are, not who you wish they were. The more you focus on what's *right* with them, the more you'll enjoy your relationship. Love their quirks. Admire their strengths. And when you need change, invite it together, not through control. A loved person grows better than a criticized one.

 Conversation starter: What are the things you want to do before you die?

Day 198

*A great marriage is when an imperfect couple
learns to enjoy their differences.*

A great marriage isn't about finding someone who mirrors you perfectly; it's about learning to embrace the differences that make you unique as a couple. One of you might love spontaneity while the other thrives on planning. One might be the night owl, the other an early bird. Instead of letting those contrasts frustrate you, choose to see them as balance. Your differences can make you stronger, bringing perspectives, skills, and energy the other doesn't have. A great marriage isn't about erasing imperfections, it's about laughing at them, learning from them, and enjoying the quirky blend that only the two of you create together.

Day 199

*Marriage is a workshop... where one spouse works
and the other spouse shops.*

Okay, it's a joke—but there's a little truth wrapped in the humor. Every marriage has its own unique rhythms, roles, and inside jokes. The key? Balance and appreciation. If one of you is always working while the other spends freely, resentment may build. But when both feel seen, heard, and free to enjoy life, it works. Find what "balance" looks like for your unique relationship. And keep laughing. Humor is a hidden superpower in marriage.

 Something to talk about: What are our plans for purchasing a home?

Day 200

Morning snuggles can be the best way to start the day.

Morning snuggles can be the best way to start the day, not just because they're cozy, but because they create a moment of connection before the world rushes in. In that sleepy space between dreams and deadlines, you have a chance to be present, to hold each other without distraction, and to remind your partner, "You're my safe place." It doesn't have to be long—just a few extra minutes of closeness can shift the tone of the whole day. Before the texts, the to-do lists, the coffee, there's "us." And sometimes, that soft, quiet start is exactly what love needs to stay strong.

Day 201

Marriage is like farming, constantly planting, growing, and harvesting.

No matter how great yesterday was, today requires fresh effort. Like a farmer tending their fields, marriage thrives on daily investment. You wake up every day and choose patience, kindness, communication, and forgiveness over and over again. Crops don't grow without water, and love doesn't deepen without attention. There will be dry spells and rainy days, but consistency yields fruit. It's tempting to coast on good days, but real love is built on the ordinary, intentional ones. Every morning presents an opportunity to sow peace, pull weeds, and cultivate joy. The harvest? A strong, thriving relationship you've nurtured together.

 Ask each other: What are three things that irritate you about me?

105

Day 202

Marriage isn't something you get; it's something you do.

Love is a choice you keep making, not just a one-time vow. Marriage isn't a possession; it's a practice. It shows up in how you speak, how you listen, and how you keep showing up even on days you don't feel like it. It's expressed in patience, affection, and those quiet moments of kindness that no one else sees. You don't just *have* a good marriage, you build one, moment by moment, act by act. So, treat love as a verb. It's not a finish line; it's a walk you take together, one day at a time.

Day 203

Never seek relationship advice from someone
who has never been married.

Never seek relationship advice from someone who has never been married, because experience matters. Marriage is its own unique journey, filled with compromises, daily choices, and challenges you can't fully understand until you've experienced them. Friends who've never worn the ring may mean well, but their advice often lacks the nuance that comes from walking through both the highs and the lows of partnership. One exception? Trusted clergy or counselors, who may not be married themselves but have guided countless couples through the ups and downs. Still, when possible, lean on the wisdom of those who have lived what you're stepping into. Their perspective is tested, grounded, and rooted in reality, and that makes it invaluable.

 Conversation starter: How do you feel about marriage counseling?

Day 204

Do not expect your spouse to change after you're married.

If you're banking on marriage to transform a partner's habits, you may be setting yourself up for frustration. That pile of laundry on the chair? That "I'll do it later" attitude? Expect it to come with you into married life. Love someone for who they are now, not who you think you can mold them into. People *can* grow, but it has to be their choice. Entering marriage with clear eyes and open hearts means embracing the flaws alongside the fun. If something really bothers you, talk about it, but don't expect a wedding ring to work magic.

Day 205

On the flip side, everyone changes.

While you may hope your spouse never changes, the truth is they will. Life brings physical, emotional, and spiritual changes, and marriage doesn't freeze time. The person you marry will continue to grow, shift, and evolve. And that's a good thing. Expecting your spouse to stay the same is not only unrealistic, it's unfair. Learn to celebrate who they are becoming, not just who they were. Be curious. Ask questions. Offer support instead of resistance. A lasting marriage isn't about holding each other, it's about learning how to move forward side by side, even as you both become new versions of yourselves.

 Ask each other: What is your favorite childhood memory?

Day 206

No new pets the first year.

As cute and cuddly as a puppy or kitten might be, adding a new responsibility in your first year of marriage can backfire. The first year is for figuring out each other's rhythms, routines, and how to communicate under one roof. A pet can introduce stress, mess, and added pressure before you've fully found your footing as a couple. Give yourselves time to settle in and enjoy each other without extra demands. The dog can wait. The marriage needs training first. And when you do decide the time is right, you'll be better prepared to handle the chaos with teamwork instead of tension.

Day 207

No, your spouse doesn't want to smell that!

Your spouse isn't your college roommate or the buddy you swap fart jokes with, so treat them differently. Love might be unconditional, but that doesn't mean basic courtesy goes out the window. Keep a few habits to yourself, especially the ones involving smells, sounds, or bodily "expressions." Comfort and closeness don't mean giving up on boundaries. A little personal hygiene and a touch of mystery can go a long way in keeping attraction alive. Remember, you're sharing a life, not trying to gross each other out. Love doesn't mean losing all filters; it means respecting the space you both call home. So, light a candle, crack a window, and maybe keep the fart jokes to yourself.

 Conversation starter: In what ways do we overshare as a couple?

Day 208

Your job can hurt your relationship, don't let it.

Work is important, but it can quietly erode your connection if you're not careful. Late nights, stress, and burnout can spill over into your home life, leaving little energy for your partner. Set boundaries where you can and communicate about your workload. Prioritize each other in the margins of your day. Your career might pay the bills, but your relationship is what makes it all worthwhile. Don't let your best energy go to the office and leave your partner with the scraps. Love is a job, too. It deserves your time and attention.

Day 209

*If your spouse suddenly seems off, assume
they need your help, not your criticism.*

Not every off mood is a slight against you. Sometimes your partner's silence, irritability, or distance has nothing to do with you, and everything to do with something heavy they're carrying. Lead with compassion, not correction. Instead of asking, "What's wrong with you?" try, "What can I do for you?" or even offer a quiet presence. A loving response creates a sense of safety, which in turn builds trust, ultimately strengthening the bond. Criticism adds weight. Support lightens the load. You're on the same team, so be the soft place they can land, especially when the world outside isn't giving them much room to breathe.

 Something to talk about: If you're in a funk, what is the best way to support you?

Day 210

Jealousy destroys relationships.

Jealousy destroys relationships, not all at once, but slowly, quietly, and deeply. It chips away at trust, breeds insecurity, and turns love into suspicion. What begins as a glance or a harmless comment can spiral into assumptions, accusations, and control. And that's no foundation for intimacy. Healthy love is built on freedom, not fear. It says, "I choose you," not "I own you." If jealousy creeps in, don't ignore it, talk about it, and figure out where it's coming from. Often, it stems from self-doubt, not your partner's behavior. Work on trust, both in them and in yourself, because love can't thrive where it's constantly questioned. Choose curiosity over control and openness over assumption.

Day 211

Never "borrow" your partner's earbuds.

Headphones or earbuds might not look like a big deal, but for many, they're prized possessions. If you borrow them "just for a quick run" and return them sweaty, tangled, or with your playlist still queued up, don't be surprised if your partner looks personally offended. It's not about the earbuds themself; it's about respect for the things your partner treasures. In marriage, honoring these small boundaries goes a long way. Protect the little things, and you build trust for the bigger ones.

 Ask each other: What is the one thing or person you are jealous of? Why?

Day 212

Laugh with each other, never at each other.

Laughter is one of the sweetest forms of intimacy. It creates joy, eases tension and pulls you closer. But it's a fragile thing when it turns the wrong way. Be careful with jokes at your partner's expense, especially in public. What might seem funny to you could land as a sting to them. Inside jokes? Great. Shared silliness? Beautiful. But keep it loving. Laugh together, not apart. Marriage should feel like a safe space for your quirks and missteps, not a stage for sarcastic punchlines. Choose humor that lifts, not wounds, because the best kind of love knows when to laugh and when to protect.

Day 213

*Learn to like (or at least appreciate) a hobby
that your spouse loves.*

You don't have to become an expert in their favorite pastime but showing interest in what lights them up is an act of love. Maybe it's hiking, gaming, gardening, or watching documentaries about obscure historical figures. You don't have to love the *thing*, but loving that it brings them joy? That matters. Ask questions. Try it once. Sit beside them while they do it. These shared moments, both big or small, create connection. And who knows? You might even surprise yourself. When you step into each other's worlds, you're saying: "What matters to you matters to me."

 Conversation starter: What is one hobby you tried before and want to try again?

Day 214

Discuss parenthood in depth before having children.

Take the time to talk through as much as possible before having kids, because it's one of the most important conversations you'll ever have. Parenting isn't just about names and nursery colors; it's about values, discipline styles, responsibilities, finances, and protecting your relationship while raising a family. Discuss how you'll handle sleepless nights, childcare, education, holidays, and even screen time. You can't plan for everything, but going into parenthood with a shared understanding and united front will give you a stronger foundation. The more you prepare now, the better you'll navigate the surprises later.

Day 215

Make big decisions together.

Not all "big decisions" look the same to both of you. One might think buying a car is a major decision; the other feels the same about rearranging the living room. Before making joint calls, talk about what each of you considers a big deal. Set a foundation: "Let's always check in before..." That clarity prevents accidental hurt and unnecessary tension. Making decisions together is more than logistics; it's about honoring each other's voice. When both people feel heard, seen, and consulted, you're not just managing life, you're building it hand in hand. That's the heart of a healthy partnership.

 Something to talk about: Public, private, or home school for the kids?

Day 216

Make sure to hug or kiss each other daily.

It sounds simple, but consistent physical affection builds powerful connection. A daily hug or kiss says, "I see you," "I choose you," and "We're still in this together." Don't save it for special occasions. Let it be a ritual when you wake up, leave the house, come home, or go to bed. These small acts nourish your bond more than grand gestures ever could. They're reminders in motion that say, "You're loved." Life gets busy. Days get hard. But one moment of physical touch can reset your rhythm and remind you both: love lives here.

Day 217

If you need to talk about your sex life, do so outside of the bedroom.

Sex is a vital part of intimacy, but it can also be a vulnerable topic. If something needs to be said, such as more connection, less pressure, different desires, choose a calm, neutral time to talk. Don't bring conflict into the bedroom. That space should feel safe, not stressful. Treat the conversation with care and mutual respect. It's not about blaming, it's about growing. Check in with each other. Be honest, gentle, and open. A healthy sex life isn't just about frequency or technique, it's about emotional safety, trust, and shared joy. Make space for honesty *and* tenderness.

 Ask each other: What is something you'd like to change or add to our sex life?

Day 218

Make your sexual relationship a high priority.

In the whirlwind of jobs, chores, and responsibilities, sex can quietly slide to the bottom of the list, but it's worth keeping close to the top. Intimacy deepens connection, releases tension and reminds you both that you're not just roommates. Prioritizing sex doesn't mean turning it into a task; it means honoring it as a meaningful part of your relationship. Be intentional. Make time, not just space. Keep the spark alive with flirtation, affection, and playfulness. And remember, it's not just about the physical act, it's about feeling desired, seen, and cherished.

Day 219

Marriage is often the hardest thing you'll ever do.

Marriage can be difficult, not because something's wrong, but because building a life with another person takes work, patience, and determination. It's waking up beside someone who sometimes frustrates you and choosing to love anyway. It's about learning to communicate through conflict, growing through seasons of change, and staying when staying feels like the harder choice. Marriage reveals your strengths, your flaws, and everything in between. But here's the truth: the hardest things are often the most meaningful. When you fight for each other, not against each other, you build something real and resilient.

 Conversation starter: How do you feel about scheduling intimate time when life gets busy?

Day 220

May all your ups and downs be in bed!

Marriage comes with plenty of ups and downs, but the best ones are the playful kind that happen between the sheets. Humor and intimacy go hand in hand, keeping things light, fun, and connected reminds you that passion is as important as partnership. Life will bring challenges outside the bedroom, so let the bedroom be the place where you recharge, laugh, and enjoy each other. A healthy sex life doesn't just add spark, it builds closeness, relieves stress, and strengthens the bond that carries you through everything else. Here's to making sure your favorite highs and lows happen under the covers.

Day 221

Your bedroom should be a sanctuary.

Your bedroom should be a sanctuary, not a battleground. It's where you rest, recharge, and reconnect, not where hard conversations should unfold. When serious issues arise, especially those related to intimacy or conflict, find a neutral and calm space. A walk, the living room, or even a quiet car ride can work. This separation helps protect your bedroom energy and ensures conversations happen with clarity, not emotional overload. Talking in neutral spaces encourages resolution instead of reactivity. Guard your bedroom like a sacred space for connection, not confrontation. What happens there should always feel safe, never strained.

 Something to talk about: Can we agree, no screens in the bedroom?

Day 222

*Never make your spouse responsible for
your own happiness.*

Your partner can love you, support you, encourage you, but they can't *complete* you. That's your job. Expecting someone else to make you happy every day is an impossible ask and an unfair burden. Take ownership of your joy. Nurture your own interests, friendships, and well-being. A healthy marriage is made up of two whole people, not two halves hoping the other will fill in their blanks. When you bring happiness into the relationship instead of just pulling it from it, everything feels lighter, freer, and more fulfilling. Love grows best when it's not weighed down by unrealistic expectations.

Day 223

Never say "I Love You" out of routine.

"I love you" are three little words that carry significant weight. They're not just punctuation for a phone call or filler before sleep. When said with meaning, they anchor your connection and remind your partner that they're truly seen and valued. But when the words become automatic, they risk losing their spark. Don't let love get lazy. Say it when your heart feels full, when your spouse does something small but wonderful, or even in the middle of a hard moment, especially then. Look them in the eye. Let it land. Love deserves to be spoken with intention, not habit.

 Ask each other: What's your ideal way to spend a lazy day at home together?

Day 224

Don't just say, "I love you," show "I love you," with small, intentional acts of love.

Love isn't just something you declare; it's something you *do*. It's pouring the coffee the way they like it. It's rubbing their shoulders after a long day. It's remembering their favorite snack at the grocery store or leaving a note on the bathroom mirror before a big meeting. These simple, thoughtful gestures whisper, *I believe in you. I care. I'm still choosing you.* Showing up for your partner in meaningful ways, especially when it's not expected, makes love feel alive and felt, not just heard. Say the words, but back them up with action.

Day 225

You must work daily to keep love, romance, and marriage alive.

Love doesn't just coast along. It needs motion, like small gestures, thoughtful words, and intentional connection. Romance isn't reserved for Valentine's Day or anniversary dinners, it's built in the ordinary day to day moments. It's remembering their favorite snack, reaching for their hand, sending a midday "thinking of you" text. Marriage, like anything worth keeping, takes care. Don't let routine dull your passion. Stir the pot with surprise and sweetness. This isn't pressure, it's power. You *get* to choose each other every day.

 Ask each other: What do you think we'll be doing 10, 20, 30, 40 years from now?

Day 226

Set an annual couple's goal.

Set an annual couple's goal, something you dream up together that keeps you moving forward as a team. It can be big or small: saving for a trip, starting a new tradition, learning a skill together, or even committing to more unplugged time each week. The point isn't perfection: it's shared intention. Life gets busy, and it's easy to slip into autopilot. A yearly goal provides a clear target to work toward, celebrate, and track progress throughout the year. It's a way to stay aligned, to grow side by side, and to keep your relationship fresh and forward focused. When you chase something together, even the effort becomes a connection.

Day 227

Nurture your identity as a couple, as well as an individual.

Nurture your identity as a couple but also protect time to be your own person. Go on date nights, plan shared goals, and enjoy building a life together, but don't stop doing the things that light you up. Continue to see your friends, pursue your hobbies, and invest in your personal growth. If you love hiking and your partner doesn't, go anyway. If they thrive in a book club or on solo runs, cheer them on. Encourage one another to continue evolving, not just as partners, but as individuals. Then bring that growth back into the relationship. The healthiest couples make space for both connection and independence.

 Conversation starter: What annual trips do you like to take?

Day 228

Love is a choice.

Feelings come and go. Some days, love feels like fireworks; other days, it's more like fog. But true love is less about how you feel and more about how you show up. It's in the daily choices to be kind, to forgive, to stay when it's hard, and to listen when you'd rather check out. Love is a decision to see your partner with grace, even when they're not at their best. You won't always *feel* in love, but you can always *choose* love. Over time, that choice creates something deeper, stronger, and more enduring than fleeting emotions ever could.

Day 229

Nobody's perfect. Cut your spouse some slack!

We're all a work in progress, and your spouse is no exception. But neither are you. Before jumping to frustration or judgment, remember that grace goes both ways. Everyone has off days, annoying habits, and moments they wish they could rewind. Love means offering compassion in the moment, not just in hindsight. So, when the toothpaste cap is missing or they forget the thing you reminded them about five times, just breathe and laugh if you can. Your relationship isn't built on perfection; it's built on patience, understanding, and a whole lot of grace.

 Something to talk about: What is the best or worst trait you inherited from your parents?

Every season of love asks for something new, and every season gives something back.

Chapter 5

Communication & Conflict
Use your words, but still be kind

Day 230

---

*Go over, go under, go around, or go through,
but never give up.*

Marriage will test your creativity, patience, and perseverance. There will be moments when things feel stuck, when communication falters, and when life throws more at you than you think you can handle. That's when this mindset matters most. Not every challenge has a clear path forward, but there *is* always a path. Perhaps it's having a difficult conversation, adjusting expectations, seeking assistance, or simply taking a moment to regroup. What matters is that you keep choosing each other, even if it's messy or uncertain. Giving up might seem easier in the moment, but working through it strengthens not just your bond but your belief in what you've built. Love isn't about smooth roads; it's about resilience. So, when you hit a wall, don't retreat. Reroute. Dig deep. Try again. The couples who last aren't the ones who never struggle; they're the ones who refuse to quit on each other.

 Conversation starter: When we hit challenges, how can we remind ourselves we're on the same team?

Day 231

Choose your battles wisely.

In marriage, you'll face countless little annoyances, differing opinions, and mismatched habits. But before jumping into an argument, ask yourself: *"Is this really worth it?"* Will it matter tomorrow, or are you just tired, stressed, or craving control? Some things deserve a conversation. Others deserve a deep breath and a sense of humor. You don't have to address every sock on the floor or every mispronounced word at dinner. Let the small stuff go when you can. Save your energy for the things that truly matter to your connection, values, or well-being. Peace isn't passive, it's intentional. And knowing when to speak up versus when to let it slide is one of the quietest forms of wisdom in marriage.

Day 232

Don't continue to argue just to prove you're right.

Arguments aren't competitions; they're conversations with emotion. When voices rise and tensions flare, it's easy to lose sight of what really matters. Winning the fight shouldn't be the goal— finding connection and understanding should be. Stay calm. Take a breath. Pause if needed. If you keep going just to be "right," you might say something you regret or damage trust in the process. A calm tone creates safety and space for resolution. Heated arguments rarely heal anything, but grounded, respectful ones can change everything. Choose clarity over chaos.

 Ask each other: When do you feel jealous?

Day 233

You'll never forgive anything once.

Forgiveness isn't a one-and-done deal, it's a process. Even after you say, "I forgive you," the hurt can resurface. And when it does, you'll have to decide again to let go, to release bitterness, and to choose peace over punishment. That doesn't mean ignoring boundaries or tolerating harm. It means refusing to let past pain poison your present. Forgiveness is love in action, again and again. It's not forgetting; it's choosing freedom over resentment, and that choice often has to be made more than once. Some days, it's an hourly decision. That's okay.

Day 234

Admit when you're wrong.

There's nothing more disarming than a genuine apology. Saying "I was wrong" isn't a sign of weakness; it's a mark of maturity. It shows that your pride doesn't matter more than your partner's peace. We all mess up. However, owning your mistakes builds trust, fosters repair, and strengthens connection. The longer you delay the admission, the bigger the damage. Lead with humility and take responsibility without defensiveness. It might sting your ego in the moment, but it strengthens your relationship for the long haul. A heartfelt "I'm sorry" can turn a fight into a fresh start.

 Conversation starter: Do you believe forgiveness is a one-time act or an ongoing choice?

Day 235

Ask yourself: Do you want to be happy or be right?

You can be right and still be lonely. Sometimes we get so caught up in making our case that we bulldoze over our partner's feelings. Yes, facts matter, but so does empathy. Ask yourself, is being "right" more important than being connected? Winning the argument might feel good in the moment, but long-term happiness comes from choosing love over ego. Be willing to listen, to compromise, and to let small stuff slide. When you choose peace over pride, you both win. The healthiest relationships are built on harmony, not victory.

Day 236

It's how you argue that matters.

Disagreements are part of any relationship. You're two different people with two different brains, so it's inevitable. What matters isn't if you argue, but how. Do you listen? Do you respect each other? Do you fight to fix, not to wound? Fighting fair means using calm words, not insults. Staying present, not storming out. Fighting with the goal of repair, not revenge. Healthy couples fight, then grow closer from the resolution. So don't fear conflict. Just learn to do it with care, honesty, and love. And remember, you don't always have to agree to move forward, you just need to understand each other.

 Ask each other: How did the way your parents handle conflict shape how you handle conflict today?

Day 237

Fights are not an acceptable form of communication.

Yelling, slamming doors, and cold shoulders may release emotions, but they rarely lead to resolution. Healthy communication requires calm, clear, and honest conversations. If something's bothering you, speak up before it turns into a fight. Choose timing, tone, and words with care. Instead of reacting, try responding. Communication is a bridge, not a battleground. When couples learn to discuss their issues rather than fighting them, they build a relationship that feels safe, supportive, and strong. Conflict is natural. Communication is learned. The first is inevitable. The second is your superpower.

Day 238

Honesty always... but not as a weapon or to cause harm.

Honesty is vital, but it's not a license to be harsh. Truth, when delivered with cruelty, becomes a weapon. Share your thoughts with care and compassion. Consider your partner's feelings and the context before you speak. Ask yourself: is this helpful? Necessary? Kind? Honesty should build trust, not shatter confidence. If you're using "truth" as an excuse to be mean, you're missing the point. Love speaks truth with gentleness, especially when it's hard. Be brave enough to be honest and wise enough to be tender while doing it.

 Something to talk about: Some people kiss and make up after an argument. What should our 'thing' be?

Day 239

In disagreements, don't bring up old baggage.

When you're upset, it's tempting to dig through the archives and throw past wrongs into the current argument. But bringing up old baggage only clouds the issue and escalates tension. Stay focused on the present moment. Deal with the conflict at hand without dragging in unresolved frustrations from last month, or last year. If those old wounds still hurt, address them at another time. Fighting fair means not stockpiling grievances to use as ammo. Keep the conversation clean, specific, and respectful. You can't move forward if you're always looking back.

Day 240

In disagreements, never lose the lesson.

Every conflict holds a lesson about your partner, your triggers, your communication style, or your unmet needs. Instead of seeing arguments as failures, view them as opportunities to understand each other better. Once the storm has passed, reflect together: What did we learn? What can we do differently next time? Healthy couples use disagreements to build bridges, not walls. When you're willing to find meaning in the mess, you strengthen your connection and grow closer. Don't just survive the disagreement, learn from it because that's how love evolves.

 Ask each other: How can I love you better on hard days?

Day 241

It's better to tell a hurtful truth than a comforting lie.

Trust can't survive on half-truths or sugarcoated silence. In marriage, honesty is the foundation of a strong and intimate relationship. It's not always easy to say what needs to be said, especially when you know it might sting. But lies, even well-meaning ones, create cracks that widen over time. A hard truth, delivered with care, shows respect for your partner and your relationship. It says, "I trust you enough to be real with you." Comforting lies may feel easier in the moment, but they erode trust in the long run. Speak with love and honesty, not with cruelty.

Day 242

Secrets don't stay buried for long.

Secrets don't stay buried for long—not in marriage, not in life. What's hidden eventually finds its way to the surface, often at the worst possible time. Whether it's a financial decision, a past mistake, or something left unsaid, keeping secrets creates a silent barrier between you and your partner. It chips away at trust, and over time, even the smallest secrets can grow heavy. Honesty may feel uncomfortable during the moment, but it's far easier than the damage caused when the truth comes out later. A strong relationship can weather hard conversations, but it struggles to survive deception. If something's weighing on you, share it. Say it with care— but say it.

 Conversation starter: What significant event changed you?

Day 243

Never say anything deliberately cruel.

Words can leave wounds that don't show up on skin but cut just as deep. In moments of anger, it can be tempting to say something sharp or go for the emotional jugular, but cruelty doesn't solve conflict. It creates shame, insecurity, and fear. You know your partner's soft spots, and they know yours, so treat that knowledge with care, even in arguments. Being upset doesn't give you a free pass to be mean. Love doesn't withhold the truth, but it does deliver it with respect. Choose your words with intention. Once spoken, they can't be unsaid.

Day 244

Never say, "I told you so."

Even if you were right—especially if you were right—resist the urge to gloat. "I told you so" might feel like a victory, but it creates embarrassment, shame, and division. Your relationship is not a scoreboard, and proving a point shouldn't come at the cost of your partner's dignity. In moments when they're already frustrated or disappointed, offer support instead of smugness. Let them come to you for comfort, not criticism. It's better to be a soft landing than a loud reminder. Being right is rarely as important as being kind. Stay humble, even when the facts are on your side.

 Ask each other: What is the one thing about your past you are afraid to tell anyone?

Day 245

The best way out of a problem is straight through.

Avoiding conflict doesn't make it disappear; it just delays the inevitable. And by the time it resurfaces, it's often grown into something bigger. The only real way out of a challenge is through honest conversation, patience, and problem-solving together. Lean into discomfort. Face the tension head-on. It won't always be easy, but it will move you forward. Sweeping things under the rug only builds resentment and distance. Your love is strong enough to weather storms, but only if you both commit to walking through them, hand in hand.

Day 246

The first to forgive is the strongest; the first to forget is the happiest.

Forgiveness isn't weakness, it's courage in its purest form. It takes strength to let go of the need to be right, to release resentment, and to choose love over pride. However, once forgiveness is given, true freedom comes from choosing not to carry the weight of the past. Forgetting doesn't mean pretending it never happened; it means not letting it control your present. It's choosing peace over replaying the hurt. In a strong marriage, both partners are likely to make mistakes. What matters most is how quickly you return to each other. The faster you let go of what doesn't serve your love, the more room you make for joy, trust, and healing.

 Conversation starter: What small, daily habits could we create to keep our love strong?

Day 247

There are three sides to every argument:
Side 1, Side 2, and the truth

There are three sides to every argument: your side, their side, and the truth that lives somewhere in between. In the heat of conflict, it's easy to get locked into your own perspective—what you felt, what you meant, and how you were hurt. But your partner has their own experience, shaped by emotions, assumptions, and history. Neither view is wrong; they're just incomplete. The real truth often lies in the overlap, in the space where both stories are heard with empathy. Instead of fighting to win, fight to *understand*. Ask questions. Listen with curiosity, not a comeback. Most arguments aren't about facts, they're about feelings. And the faster you can move from proving your point to finding common ground, the stronger your relationship will become.

Day 248

There is no delete key for the spoken word.

Words leave marks. Some soothe; others create a scar. Once said, you can't unsay them, and even an apology doesn't erase the memory. In moments of frustration, it's tempting to blurt out whatever's on your mind. But your partner deserves more than your unfiltered emotions. Pause. Ask yourself if your words are true, necessary, and kind. If they aren't, it's okay to wait. Silence can be a gift if it protects the relationship while you process. Remember, you can repair a lot, but you can't rewind.

 Ask each other: What's something you hope never changes between us?

Day 249

"We have two ears and one mouth so that we can listen twice as much as we speak." — Epictetus

Listening may not sound exciting, but it's one of the most effective relationship tools available. Real listening isn't just nodding while you plan what to say next; it's actually *hearing* your partner. It's leaning in, asking follow-up questions, and showing them that they matter. Sure, talking feels good, but listening is what builds trust. When you tune in, you create a space where honesty feels safe and connection grows stronger. Slow down, take a breath, and just *listen*. Sometimes the greatest gift you can give is your full attention, without rushing to fix or respond.

Day 250

Yelling and screaming never solves a thing.

You might feel better in the moment, but raising your voice rarely leads to resolution; it usually just raises defenses. The louder you shout, the less your partner can hear you, and the more the issue gets buried beneath emotion. Conflict doesn't need volume, it needs clarity. If things get heated, take a breath, step away, and revisit the conversation when you can both speak calmly. You're not enemies trying to win, you're partners trying to understand. Lower the volume, raise the respect, and watch how much more progress you make.

 Something to talk about: Did your parents yell and scream during your childhood?

Day 251

*The power of touch is amazing and can
heal better than words.*

Words matter, but touch can say, "I still choose you" in a way language can't always capture. After an argument, once you've talked it out, reconnect physically—even if it's just a hug or a gentle hand on the shoulder. That small gesture rebuilds trust and reminds you both that your bond is stronger than disagreement. Reconciliation isn't just about resolving issues; it's about returning to each other. Let touch speak where words pause. And yes, that "kiss and make up" cliché? Totally underrated.

Day 252

Show your love by choosing to yield in a disagreement.

In every partnership, there will be moments when standing your ground feels justified. But sometimes, yielding is the stronger move. It's saying, "I hear you. I care more about us than winning this point." When you release the need to be right and instead lean into compassion, you create space for trust and connection to grow. Yielding doesn't mean silencing your voice; it means knowing when compromise brings more peace than pushing forward. Love isn't proven in big, dramatic moments; it's built in quiet decisions, when you choose grace over ego and unity over being right.

 Conversation starter: What does partnership mean to you, and how can I be a better partner?

Day 253

Guard each other's secrets.

What your partner tells you in confidence should stay there. Being their safe space means protecting their vulnerability, even when it's tempting to share a story or vent to someone else. Whether it's a fear, a family detail, or something embarrassing, treat their trust like gold. Relationships thrive on emotional safety, and once it's broken, it's hard to rebuild. Make it a rule between you: what's shared between us, stays with us. Loyalty isn't just about staying faithful, it's about protecting the private pieces of your partner's heart.

Day 254

Discuss finances often to make sure you're still on the same page.

Money stress can quietly wreak havoc in a relationship if you're not checking in regularly. Don't wait until a credit card is maxed out or a big purchase causes a blow-up. Schedule low-stress money talks, such as weekly or monthly check-ins where you talk about spending, saving, and goals. Be honest about your habits and open to compromise. Transparency builds trust, and teamwork builds success. Budgeting isn't sexy, but knowing you're aligned on finances takes pressure off your day-to-day. A shared financial vision is just as intimate as any other plan you make together.

 Ask each other: Do you think there is such a thing as "good debt?"

Day 255

Distrust is a slippery slope.

All it takes is one unanswered question, one hidden truth, or one unexplained change in behavior to send your partner's imagination spiraling. Trust takes time to build, but it can be shattered in seconds. Keep your words consistent with your actions. Be open, even about uncomfortable topics. When your partner feels secure in your honesty, there's no need to fill in blanks with worst-case scenarios. But when you're vague or evasive, doubt creeps in. If you make a mistake, own up to it quickly. It's easier to rebuild a stumble than repair a fall.

Day 256

Never use tears to manipulate.

Emotions are real, and tears are valid, but when they're used to guilt, control, or shift blame, they become a tool, not a truth. In a healthy relationship, vulnerability should invite connection, not compliance. If you're crying, let it be because you feel deeply, not because you're trying to steer the outcome. And if you notice you're leaning on tears to avoid accountability or dodge a hard conversation, pause and check in with yourself. Manipulation, even unintentional, can damage trust over time. Tears can be powerful, but their power lies in honesty, not in strategy.

 Something to talk about: What's something about our relationship you're proud of?

Day 257

Don't be afraid to disagree.

Disagreement doesn't mean you're doomed, it just means you're two individuals with opinions, values, and preferences. And that's healthy. Avoiding conflict for the sake of "peace" often leads to unspoken resentment. The key is to disagree respectfully. Listen fully. Express yourself clearly. Assume good intent. When handled with care, disagreement sharpens communication, fosters growth, and deepens understanding. You don't need to agree on everything; you just need to decide on how to disagree well. Marriage isn't about sameness; it's about finding unity in the midst of difference.

Day 258

Don't become resentful of your partner if you've dragged them somewhere they don't want to be.

Don't become resentful of your partner if you've dragged them somewhere they didn't want to be. If you invited them to that party, yoga class, or weekend getaway they weren't thrilled about, remember, it was your idea. Expecting them to be instantly enthusiastic might be setting the bar unfairly high. People show up in different ways, and just because they're not grinning ear to ear doesn't mean they're not trying. Appreciate the effort, not just the energy. If you pressure them to go, don't punish them for not loving it. Instead, meet them with gratitude, not attitude.

 Conversation starter: How can we stay connected when we disagree?

Day 259

Your partner can't fix what they don't know is wrong.

We all rehearse arguments in our heads, but assuming your partner *should* know why you're upset only creates distance. You might be annoyed, frustrated, or hurt, but if you're not saying it out loud, you're not giving them a chance to change it. Don't let unspoken expectations fester. Say what you need, kindly and clearly. Chances are that your partner would rather know than guess. Most hurt feelings don't come from malicious intent, they come from miscommunication. Let them in. You'll probably be surprised how willing they are to fix what they didn't know was broken.

Day 260

Don't just tell your spouse you love them,
tell them <u>why</u> you love them.

"I love you" is powerful, but after a while, it can become a habit said more out of routine than revelation. Spice it up by telling your partner *why*. "I love how patient you are with my family." "I love the way your eyes crinkle when you laugh." "I love that you bring me coffee without asking." Specificity deepens connection. It reminds your partner they're seen, appreciated, and valued for more than just their title in your life. Words of affirmation are strongest when they're personal. Let them know not just that you love them, but exactly why.

 Ask each other: What does "choosing each other every day" look like to you?

Day 261

Don't keep secrets from one another and don't lie - ever!

A single lie, even a "small" one, can plant seeds of doubt that grow into full-blown distrust. Secrets make your partner feel excluded—and exclusion erodes intimacy. Transparency keeps you connected. If you feel like you need to hide something, ask yourself why. What fear is driving the secrecy? Then face it together. Marriage thrives on safety, and safety starts with truth. No matter how uncomfortable a conversation may be, it's always better than deception. Tell the truth the first time. It's far less painful than the fallout from a broken bond.

Day 262

*Even a little white lie will come back to haunt
you over and over.*

Even a little white lie will come back to haunt you, often at the worst possible time. It may seem harmless in the moment, a way to keep the peace or avoid conflict, but even small untruths plant seeds of doubt. Once trust is broken, it's hard to repair fully. Your partner might not catch it right away, but if (or when) the truth surfaces, it can make them question what else hasn't been real. Honesty isn't always the easiest route, but it's the one that builds lasting security. If something feels hard to say, that's often a sign it *needs* to be said. Tell the truth with kindness.

 Conversation starter: How can we ensure there is a safe space in our marriage to remain honest with each other?

Day 263

Ask your spouse what you can do to better this week.

Sometimes love shows up in the smallest gestures, such as a chore done without being asked, a lunch packed before work, or giving your partner space when they're overwhelmed. Asking, "What can I do to make this week easier?" opens the door to connection, service, and teamwork. It's not about grand romantic gestures; it's about everyday support. When you ask this regularly, you show your partner that their well-being matters to you. You're choosing to be proactive, not reactive. Marriage is built in weeks, not decades, so tend to the days in front of you, and your forever will take care of itself.

Day 264

Show compassion often, so your partner feels safe being honest when it really matters.

When your partner knows, they can come to you with hard truths and be met with grace, not rage, you create an environment of emotional safety. That doesn't mean you condone poor behavior, but it means you keep your reactions grounded in love, not punishment. Relationships thrive when confession is met with conversation, not condemnation. Show your partner you're a safe place to land, even when it's uncomfortable. Because let's face it: mistakes will happen. But if they trust you to handle the truth with compassion, they'll tell you *before* the damage gets worse.

 Ask each other: What can I do to make this week easier?

Day 265

Fight naked!

Okay, this one's cheeky—but also surprisingly wise. The idea? Vulnerability. You can't armor up emotionally when you're completely exposed. It's hard to keep shouting when you're standing there with nothing but your pride. Whether you take this literally or symbolically, the point is to lower your defenses. Approach conflict with openness, softness, and a touch of humor when possible. Arguing isn't about tearing each other down—it's about understanding each other better. And if you can diffuse the tension with a bit of nudity or laughter? Even better. Emotional intimacy often follows physical disarmament.

Day 266

Find a marriage mentor to share your struggles.

You don't have to figure it all out on your own. Seek out a couple who are a few steps ahead of you; people who've weathered some storms, made their mistakes, and still love each other deeply. A good marriage mentor can provide wisdom, reassurance, and perspective that's hard to see from the inside. Just make sure they're trustworthy, nonjudgmental, and want to see your relationship succeed. Everyone needs a sounding board now and then and learning from others can save you from pitfalls they've already navigated.

 Something to talk about: If we were to have a marriage mentor, who would you suggest?

Day 267

*Find out early what makes your partner tick,
ticked and tickled.*

The more you understand your partner's wiring, the stronger your connection becomes. Know what brings them joy, what stresses them out, and what makes them light up with laughter. These insights help you love them better, fight smarter, and reconnect quicker. Ask questions. Pay attention. Be a student of their moods, dreams, and triggers. This isn't about walking on eggshells, it's about honoring what makes them, *them*. When you show that you care enough to know the nuances, your partner feels seen, safe, and deeply loved.

Day 268

*Give each other space: some need a closet,
others need the whole room.*

Not everyone recharges the same way. One of you might need just a few minutes to reset, while the other needs hours of solitude. That's not a rejection, it's a rhythm. Respecting each other's need for space is crucial for peace and individual growth. If your partner asks for space, give it without guilt. And if you need it, ask for it with love, not distance. The trick is not to take it personally. A little room to breathe creates more energy for togetherness. Love thrives when freedom and closeness exist side by side.

 Ask each other: What do you need more and less from me in the years ahead?

Day 269

If an argument gets heated, separate and collect your thoughts, then regroup and have a civil conversation.

When emotions run high, clarity runs out the door. Instead of powering through a heated argument, pause. Take space. Calm down. Regroup. A break isn't avoidance, it's wisdom. Let your nervous system settle so you can return to the conversation as partners, not opponents. Come back when you're ready to listen and speak respectfully. What feels like a fight about the dishwasher is usually about something deeper, and you can't uncover it in the middle of yelling. Press pause, breathe, then press play with a fresh perspective.

Day 270

If you are arguing how to do a task, remember, if the result won't matter in a week or a year, chill out!

Sometimes we get caught up in the method instead of the mission. Whether it's how to load the dishwasher or fold towels, if it won't matter in a week, or even a year, it's probably not worth a full-on conflict. Ask yourself: Is this really about the task, or is there something deeper going on? Choose your energy wisely. Peace often matters more than perfection. If the job gets done and no one loses a limb, maybe it's okay to let your partner do it their way. Let go of control, and you may gain a deeper connection.

 Conversation starter: When an argument gets intense, how do we maintain our cool?

Day 271

*If you put your problems on the back burner,
they will boil over.*

Avoidance feels safe—until it explodes. Unspoken resentments simmer quietly, but left unchecked, they bubble up in unrelated arguments, cold shoulders, or sudden distance. The longer you ignore a problem, the more powerful it becomes. Marriage is like a kitchen; don't leave pots unattended. If something's off, bring it to the table gently and sooner rather than later. It may feel easier to focus on the kids, the job, or the bills, but ignoring issues won't make them disappear. Don't let the heat build. Talk it out before it boils over and burns you both.

Day 272

*If you finish a disagreement and one of you
is not satisfied, you're not finished.*

Resolution isn't complete if someone is still quietly stewing. Just because you've moved on doesn't mean your partner has—and vice versa. Real resolution means both people feel heard, respected, and at peace. If one of you is still bothered, that's your cue to revisit the conversation with empathy and genuine curiosity. "Are we truly okay?" is a powerful question. Keep the dialogue open, not defensive. Sometimes circling back builds more trust than the initial argument ever could. Aim for mutual understanding, not just closure. Because "fine" isn't finished if someone's still hurting.

 Something to talk about: Do you agree with the idea of don't go to bed angry?

Day 273

In the grand scheme of things, it really doesn't matter if the toilet paper comes over the top or up from the bottom.

You'll face real challenges in marriage such as communication breakdowns, family drama, and financial stress.; whether your toilet paper rolls over or under should not be one of them. Some habits are just that—habits. Not hills to die on. Laugh about your quirks instead of battling them. Save your emotional energy for the issues that actually impact your relationship. And hey, if it *does* matter to one of you? Let that person win. You're not just managing a bathroom, you're building a life. Let the little things be little.

Day 274

Are there any deal-breakers in your marriage?

Some things need immediate attention. If something is lingering that's hurting your relationship—or threatening to—it's time to speak up. Silence doesn't protect love; honesty does. Whether it's a habit, an unresolved hurt, or a personal struggle, bring it into the light. Deal-breakers don't always break deals when they're faced with humility and truth. Confess, not to be punished, but to start healing. Every relationship hits rough spots but facing them together with transparency and accountability gives you the chance to rewrite the ending. Don't carry it alone. Speak it out loud so you can start to fix it together.

 Ask each other: What are your pet peeves?

Day 275

If you need to vent, let your partner know in advance that you're not looking for a fix, just compassion.

Sometimes you just want to be heard, not solved. But your partner may be wired to jump straight into "how do I fix this?" mode. That's not a flaw; it's love in action. Still, if you need someone to sit with your feelings, tell them up front: "I'm not looking for solutions right now, I just need to be heard." That little heads-up helps them show up in the right way. It's not about shutting down their instincts, it's about helping them love you the way you need in that moment. Clarity is kindness, especially during vent sessions.

Day 276

Get comfortable talking about intimate topics.

Intimacy isn't supposed to be a guessing game. Talking openly about what feels good—physically and emotionally—builds trust, closeness, and confidence. The sooner you become comfortable discussing your needs and desires, the stronger your connection will become. Shame has no place in the bedroom or the relationship. Use curiosity, gentleness, and even humor to explore together. What do you like? What don't you? What makes you feel desired? These conversations may feel awkward at first, but they create lasting safety and spark. Speak up because intimacy deepens when honesty leads the way.

 Conversation starter: Outside of sex, what are your favorite ways to be intimate?

Day 277

Meet in the middle of the conflict, the issue, the bed.

Compromise isn't just for chores and finances; it's a way of life. Whether you're facing a disagreement or a dry spell, choose to meet halfway. Not every battle needs a winner. Sometimes, choosing togetherness over being right is the best decision you'll make. And don't forget the bedroom; physical connection can bridge emotional gaps and bring you back to each other. Meet in the middle of whatever is pulling you apart. That space between "me" and "you" is where "we" happen. Relationships thrive when both people are willing to move toward each other, even when it's uncomfortable.

Day 278

Never assume your spouse knows what you're thinking.

Mind-reading isn't a language of love. Your partner can't meet a need they don't know exists. Expecting them to "just know" often leads to frustration and disappointment for both of you. Instead, express what you feel, want, and need clearly and kindly. Say the thing out loud: "I need help with this." "I'm feeling disconnected." "I'd love some time alone." When you communicate directly, you allow your partner to show up, and they often will. Love works best with instructions.

 Something to talk about: What was the last thing you kept to yourself because you didn't think I would understand?

Day 279

Sometimes it's okay to go to bed angry.

Never go to bed angry is well-known marital advice, but sometimes, honestly, it's better if you do. When you're tired, emotional, or overwhelmed, pushing for resolution can lead to more harm than healing. Sometimes the kindest thing you can do is hit pause, get some rest, and revisit the conversation with a clearer head and a softer heart. Going to bed angry doesn't mean you love each other any less—it means you're human. Just don't let the anger linger. Reconnect as soon as you can, even if it starts with a simple, "I love you, and we'll figure this out." The goal isn't to rush peace, it's to make room for it.

Day 280

Never humiliate.

Nothing wounds deeper or lingers longer than public shame from someone who's supposed to protect you. Whether it's a sarcastic joke at a dinner party or a biting comment in front of friends, humiliation cuts trust at the knees. Marriage should be a safe space, where respect is constant, not a condition. Disagreements will happen but keep them private. Build your spouse up in public. Be the one who defends, not deflates. You're on the same team, and no one wins when embarrassment is the price of a punchline.

 Conversation starter: What is the difference between poking fun and humiliating?

Day 281

Open communication is the key to making marriage work.

It sounds cliché because it's true; you can't fix what you don't talk about, and you can't connect if you're only guessing. Say the thing. Bring up what's bothering you *before* it builds into something bigger. Talk about your needs, fears, dreams, even the awkward stuff. Silence creates assumptions. Communication creates clarity. You don't need to have perfect words, just honest ones. When both people feel free to speak and safe to listen, marriage becomes a space of mutual understanding instead of a minefield. Speak often, speak early, and speak with love.

Day 282

No one can read your mind.

You may think it's obvious that you're frustrated, exhausted, or disappointed, and surely your partner can *tell*, right? But most of the time, they're just as confused as you are. Don't expect them to know what you haven't said. Clarity prevents conflict. Say what you need. Ask for what you want. Explain how you feel. Hoping they'll guess only leads to resentment and missed connection. Your partner isn't a mind reader, they're a teammate. And teammates talk. Don't bottle it up and expect magic. Speak your truth with love and invite understanding.

 Ask each other: How can we better support each other's individual dreams while growing together?

Day 283

*Oftentimes, we don't know we're making a
mistake unless we're told.*

No one gets marriage perfectly right without feedback. Your spouse can't fix what they don't know is broken. But how you bring it up matters just as much as *that* you bring it up. Approach it with grace, not blame. "I feel..." goes farther than "You always..." Offer your perspective, not a lecture. When you speak up kindly, you give your partner a chance to grow without feeling attacked. That builds trust, not tension. Your voice is valuable, but your tone gives it wings or weight. Speak with honesty, tempered by tenderness.

Day 284

*Often, the words left unspoken are the
most important ones.*

Regret often sounds like "I wish I'd told them..." Don't let love go unsaid. Don't let gratitude sit silent. The most healing, helpful, and heartwarming words are often the ones we hesitate to say. Whether it's "I'm proud of you," "I'm sorry," or "thank you for showing up every day," say it. Make your marriage a place where nothing good stays locked inside. Unspoken feelings can't grow connection. If you're thinking something kind, say it. Don't wait for a perfect moment, create one with your words.

 Something to talk about: What habits or traditions could we create now to keep our connection strong?

Day 285

Speak well of your spouse.

Your words shape how others see your partner, and how you see them, too. Make it a habit to speak positively about your spouse, especially when they're not in the room. Praise their character, not just their achievements. Brag about their kindness. Compliment their parenting. When you build them up with your words, it reinforces your love and deepens respect. It also signals to the world that this relationship matters. And let's be honest, everyone needs someone in their corner. Let your spouse know they've got the biggest cheerleader in you.

Day 286

Talk to each other, not at each other.

There's a difference. Talking *at* someone is about unloading. Talking *to* someone is about connecting. One is a monologue; the other is a dialogue. If you find yourself lecturing, commanding, or interrupting, pause and take a moment to reset. Great conversations in marriage feel like give-and-take, not give-and-get-defensive. It's okay to disagree, but do it with the goal of understanding, not domination. Slow down. Listen between the lines. Speak like you're inviting, not cornering. When you shift from a confrontational tone to a conversational one, everything changes, especially how safe and seen your spouse feels.

 Conversation starter: How do you imagine us evolving over the next five years?

Day 287

Establish mutually agreed-upon rules of engagement for arguments.

Every couple fights. But smart couples create a playbook *before* emotions run high. What are your "off-limits" words? When is it okay to pause and take a break? Can you agree not to bring up past fights during a new one? Set rules when you're calm so you'll have guidelines when you're not. This isn't about avoiding conflict; it's about protecting your connection *during* it. Think of it as setting ground rules in love's boxing ring: gloves off, hearts protected. Clear expectations reduce damage and help you both feel safer speaking your truth.

Day 288

Listen to your partner in a way that they can't possibly doubt that you love them.

Real listening is more than hearing words, it's giving someone your full presence. Put down the phone. Make eye contact. Let your partner know, "You matter right now." Listen without interrupting or preparing your rebuttal. Listen with the goal of understanding, not fixing. When someone feels deeply heard, they also feel deeply loved. You don't have to agree with everything, but you do need to care enough to listen with empathy. Be a mirror, not a megaphone. Your attention is one of the most loving gifts you can give.

 Ask each other: When we can't agree, how can we still make each other feel valued and respected?

Day 289

The secret of a happy marriage is a short tongue.

You don't have to say everything that pops into your head. Sometimes the wisest thing you can do is take a breath, pause, and *not* say that snarky comment, that comeback, or that criticism. Just because you think it doesn't mean it's helpful—or necessary. Self-control is an act of love. A short tongue isn't silence; it's discipline. It's knowing when to speak up and when to let peace be more important than proving a point. Restraint isn't a weakness; it's wisdom. And it protects what matters most: your connection.

Day 290

Be patient and do not say one negative word
to or about your spouse today.

Just for today, practice restraint and kindness as if it were a personal challenge. Even when they leave dishes in the sink or tell the same story again, no sarcasm, no sighs, no passive-aggressive digs. Zip it. Redirect. Breathe. Find the good and speak that instead. Words hold power, and one negative comment can do more damage than we realize. But a day of conscious kindness can shift the tone of your whole relationship. Positivity is a practice, and patience is its twin. One day of silence, where criticism would have been spoken, can plant seeds of peace for the whole week.

 Conversation starter: When you're having a hard day, what's the kindest thing I can do for you?

Day 291

Today, do one unexpected act of kindness for your spouse.

It doesn't need to be grand, just thoughtful. Make their coffee the way they like it. Leave a note on their pillow. Fill up their gas tank. These little surprises say, "I see you. I care." Spontaneous kindness breaks the routine and reminds your partner that they're still worth delighting. Over time, small gestures build big trust. They rekindle romance and reinforce teamwork. You don't have to wait for a birthday to go the extra mile. Ordinary Tuesday? Perfect time to bring a little joy. One act of kindness today can create a ripple of gratitude tomorrow.

Day 292

*Today, let everything you do for your spouse
come from a place of love.*

Let love be your motivation, not obligation, guilt, or habit. When you speak, let it be love talking. When you do a chore, let it be a labor of love. Even if your partner never notices the folded laundry or washed dishes, let your heart be full of generosity, not resentment. It's not about perfection, it's about intention. Love changes how you show up. It turns the mundane into meaning. Even the smallest action, when done with love, can make a mighty difference. Try it today: cook with love, talk with love, respond with love. It will show.

 Ask each other: Is there anything I do for you that you wish I wouldn't?

Day 293

*Today, make a sacrifice to lift a burden from
your spouse's shoulders.*

Marriage thrives when both people choose selflessness over convenience. Whether it's doing their least favorite chore, taking a task off their plate, or simply letting them sleep in, a small sacrifice can speak volumes. It says, "I see what you're carrying, and I want to help." Love isn't always grand gestures. Sometimes, it's stepping up in quiet ways that make your partner's day easier. You don't have to announce it or expect a gold star. Just do it because you care. Their sigh of relief? That's your reward.

Day 294

*It's just as much fun to gossip with your spouse
as it is with your friends.*

Whether it's inside jokes, shared tea, or whispered truths, your spouse should be your favorite person to dish with. Trust goes both ways: give it and guard it. If a friend shares something with confidence, keep it there. If your spouse shares something with you, protect it fiercely. When you share laughs or life updates, you build intimacy. And when you prove you're a vault, you become their safe place. Let your home be a judgment-free zone, filled with stories that remain sacred. Marriage is better when you're not just lovers, but partners in (mostly harmless) crime.

 Something to talk about: Where do you feel we've grown the most together?

Day 295

Try to see your partner's way before you say something you can't take back.

When emotions rise, it's tempting to shoot from the hip and say things that cut deep. But before you let those words fly, pause. Try to understand their perspective, their story, and their motivation. You don't have to agree, but empathy can cool a heated moment before it boils over. Ask yourself, "What might they be feeling right now?" That brief pause could save a lot of cleanup later. Because while you can apologize for harsh words, you can't always undo their impact. Lead with curiosity, not criticism.

Day 296

What counts most is how you deal with incompatibility.

No two people are perfectly matched. You may love Thai food; they may love BBQ. You might process emotions like a poet; they may need time to sort things out logically. That's okay. Love isn't built on sameness; it's built on respect and adaptability. The magic is in how you navigate the differences. Can you find a rhythm, a compromise, a shared language? Compatibility is often romanticized, but cooperation is what truly sustains. Learn to embrace the space between you as a chance to grow.

 Ask each other: Are there boundaries we need to set (or reset) with anyone in our lives?

Day 297

*What movie you watch on Friday night is NOT
a battle to be fought.*

Seriously, don't die on the hill of movie night. If one of you wants a thriller and the other wants a romantic comedy, take turns or find a hybrid. Marriage isn't about winning; it's about sharing experiences. Small decisions don't need to become power struggles. Compromise shows maturity and generosity. Let your partner choose sometimes and do it gladly, not begrudgingly. Who knows, you might discover you like the documentary you rolled your eyes at. Or you'll score points just for being a good sport. Either way, everyone wins when you learn to give a little.

Day 298

Whatever you haven't forgiven in your mate, forgive it today.

Unforgiveness is a heavy load, and dragging it around only weighs *you* down. If your partner has apologized, and you've said you forgave them, but you're still holding it over their head, it's time to truly release it. Forgiveness is a gift you give *yourself* as much as your spouse. It doesn't erase what happened, but it frees you both from the cycle of guilt and resentment. Let today be the day you say, "We're moving forward." Let go—not because they deserve it, but because peace is better than poison.

 Conversation starter: What in your life have you not yet forgiven?

Day 299

Nobody's perfect.

In the heat of frustration, it's easy to zoom in on your spouse's flaws—but pause for perspective. Are they really that bad? Probably not. They're likely trying their best in their imperfect way, just like you. Instead of spiraling into critique mode, try gratitude: "I'm mad, but I still love who they are." Reminding yourself of their goodness during conflict helps you stay grounded. It doesn't excuse the issue, but it softens your delivery. You're not arguing with a villain, you're talking to your favorite flawed human.

Day 300

When you disagree, tell your spouse how important the issue is for you on a scale of one to ten.

Not every disagreement is a hill worth dying on, but sometimes your partner won't know *how* much something matters unless you say so. Rating your level of investment helps prioritize peace. If it's a nine for you and a three for them, they'll likely yield. And if you both call it a five? You know it's worth a real conversation. This little tool helps avoid unnecessary tension and fosters mutual respect. You're not just stating your opinion, you're giving it context. That's a powerful form of honesty that keeps things productive, not personal.

 Ask each other: What is something that's a big deal for you that I don't think is important?

Day 301

Whenever you're wrong, admit it; whenever you're right, be quiet.

Humility is relationship glue. If you make a mistake, own it fully, quickly, and without excuses. But when you're right? Resist the urge to rub it in. Gloating might feel good for a second, but it creates emotional distance. Let grace lead. Being right should never be a weapon. Quiet confidence speaks louder than "I told you so." A strong relationship isn't about who wins, it's about how well you treat each other when the scoreboard tips in your favor. Choose maturity over momentary satisfaction.

Day 302

Women tend to be more emotional; men tend to be more physical. Respect the difference.

Yes, this can vary by couple, but many relationships have different emotional expressions and needs. One of you may process through conversation, the other through action, or space. It's not wrong, it's just different. Learn your partner's language. Respect their wiring, even when it confuses you. The goal isn't to change them, it's to understand and honor how they're built. Differences don't divide; they can deepen love when approached with empathy. Ask, "What helps you feel heard? What helps you feel connected?" Then listen and adjust.

 Conversation starter: How hard is it for you to admit when you're wrong, or stay humble?

Day 303

Conflict is like pouring alcohol on a wound.

Conflict isn't comfortable, but it's necessary. Like disinfecting a cut, it stings, but it also clears out the infection. Avoiding tension may feel easier in the moment, but it allows hidden hurts to fester. When you approach conflict with honesty and care, it creates space for healing. Talk it out. Say the hard thing. Listen deeply. Yes, it might hurt, but so does growth. And the result? A relationship that's not just intact, but stronger. Conflict, handled with love, becomes a doorway to deeper connection, not a death sentence.

Day 304

When you say, "I'm Sorry," look the person in the eye.

A real apology isn't just about the words; it's about presence. When you say, "I'm sorry," look into your partner's eyes. Let them see your sincerity. Let your tone, posture, and heart match your language. Eye contact invites connection. It says, "I'm here, and I care about how I've hurt you." Skimming over apologies with distracted or hurried energy robs them of their power. Take a moment. Be still. Say it with your whole self. A heartfelt "I'm sorry," offered with your eyes, can restore more than just peace—it can restore trust.

 Ask each other: What is the one thing that makes you feel like you got the better deal in our marriage?

Day 305

Never laugh at your spouse's choices; you're one of them!

It's easy to poke fun, especially when they've made a questionable outfit decision or tried to fix something with duct tape and determination. But gentle teasing can quickly turn into quiet embarrassment if it's not shared in love. Remember, the person you're joking about is the same person who chose you, quirks and all. If you're going to laugh, let it be together, not at each other. A good sense of humor is gold in marriage, but respect is the foundation. Be playful and celebrate their choices, even the odd ones, because one day, those will be the stories you tell later in life.

Day 306

A good marriage is one where each partner secretly suspects they got the better deal.

If you both feel that you've gotten the better deal, you're doing something right. It means you don't take each other for granted. You see the little things, the sacrifices, the strengths your partner brings to the relationship, and you feel lucky. Not because either of you is perfect, but because you appreciate what you have. When both people believe they've won the jackpot, it creates a foundation of gratitude, humility, and mutual admiration. So, keep noticing. Keep saying thank you. Keep showing up in ways that make your partner think, "How did I get so lucky?" Because when love is rooted in deep appreciation, it only grows stronger over time.

 Something to talk about: Can you over-do apologizing?

Day 307

Choose to react to tough circumstances in a loving way.

You don't always control what happens, but you do control how you respond. Frustration is easy; love takes intention. Next time something small goes wrong, pause before you snap. Breathe before you bite. Ask yourself, "Is this worth tension, or could it be met with grace?" Choosing love doesn't mean ignoring problems. It means responding in a way that preserves the connection, rather than pushing it away. And when you *do* mess up (because we all do), repair it with kindness. These moments build the emotional culture of your relationship; choose to build it a loving one, even on the hard days.

Day 308

Never discuss marital relationships while drinking.

Alcohol has a funny way of turning whispers into shouts and soft edges into sharp ones. It removes filters, heightens emotions, and often brings out more drama than clarity. If something serious needs to be said, save it for a sober moment. Choose calm minds and open hearts. Your marriage deserves thoughtful dialogue, not drunken reactions. Intimacy thrives on honesty, but it suffers when that honesty is blurred by drinking. Sip your wine and enjoy the moment but hit pause on the deep talks; your relationship will thank you in the morning.

 Conversation starter: What are our "ground rules' for difficult conversations?

Day 309

Never go to bed angry, even if you have to agree to disagree.

That quiet tension under the covers? It doesn't make for restful sleep or emotional closeness. Go ahead and disagree—healthy couples do—but don't let anger linger like an uninvited guest in your bed. If a resolution isn't possible right away, at least reaffirm your love. A simple, "We're not there yet, but I still care about you" can ease the tension. Conflict is normal but going to sleep emotionally disconnected chips away at intimacy over time. Choose peace over pride, even if you're not completely okay. Let your love be the last thing you share before the lights go out.

Day 310

The ideal spouse understands every word you do not say.

Some feelings live in the pauses. Some needs show up in the sighs. Emotional intelligence in marriage often looks like *noticing* not just what's said, but what's shown. Pay attention to tone, timing, and silence. When your partner withdraws, bristles, or falls quiet, don't ignore it. Gently ask, "Is there more you want to say?" You don't need to be a mind reader, just an engaged and caring observer. The best partners don't wait to be handed a script, they lean in, listen fully, and create space for what's hard to express. That kind of attentiveness is love in action.

 Ask each other: What's one word you'd want to define the next chapter of our relationship?

Day 311

*Really listen to your spouse, no matter how
absurd the problem sounds.*

Listening is one of the most loving acts you can offer, and yet it's often overlooked. Your partner's frustrations might sound small or even silly, but dismissiveness can do real damage. Don't judge. Don't fix. Just listen. Give your full attention, even if it's about printer paper, parking woes, or something that seems trivial to you. When someone feels heard, they feel valued. When they feel dismissed, they retreat. Real listening says, "You matter, even when the topic doesn't." And those few minutes? They build a bridge that holds strong when bigger storms hit.

 Conversation starter: What's a hope or dream for the future that feels a little scary to say out loud?

Chapter 6

Maintaining Happily Ever After
Love doesn't run on autopilot

Day 312

There's more to intimacy than a healthy sex life.

Intimacy is more than just physical; it's emotional, playful, and affirming. Life gets busy, kids get loud, and stress gets real, but don't let your connection slip into the background. Physical closeness matters, but so do hand-holding, lingering hugs, late-night talks, and laughing at inside jokes. Intimacy shows up in many forms, and each one feeds the bond you share.

If you've lost the spark, start by talking. Be honest, laugh about it, and take the pressure off. Connection can be rebuilt in small, consistent ways. And if intimacy feels "off" for longer than expected, don't ignore it. Hormonal changes, stress, medications, or health issues can all play a role, especially as you get older. Talking to your doctor isn't a failure—it's a way of caring for your relationship and keeping love alive.

 Conversation starter: What's something romantic (or a little naughty) you wish we did more often?

Day 313

Find other ways to express your love, such as "You're the best" and "You constantly amaze me."

Saying "I love you" daily is powerful, but adding variety keeps it fresh and deeply felt. Compliments like "You inspire me," "I admire how you handled that," or "You make my life better" hit differently. They're specific, sincere, and memorable. Your partner wants to know *why* you love them, not just *that* you do. The more you personalize your affection, the more it lands. Try a new expression of love each day. Your partner will feel appreciated and you'll both stay more connected to the reasons you chose each other in the first place.

Day 314

Learn how to say I Love You in different languages.

Why stick to one way when there are dozens of romantic ways to express love? From "Te amo" (Spanish) to "Je t'aime" (French) to "Saranghae" (Korean), each version adds a new texture to your affection. It's playful, thoughtful, and surprisingly impactful. It shows effort and creativity. Even better, learning new expressions together becomes a shared activity; it's like a private code, a sweet surprise, or even a fun inside joke. Love is a universal language, but it never hurts to say it with a twist.

 Ask each other: If we could take a class or learn a skill together, what would you want it to be?

Day 315

*All that truly matters is that you shared your
own definition of love.*

When the dust settles, the jobs end, the kids grow, and the house gets quiet, what remains is love. Not the vacations, special dinners, compromises, or who did the laundry; but the way you showed up, supported, and cherished each other. Love is the legacy. It's what people will remember. It's what *you'll* remember. Don't wait until later to live out your own special brand of love. Choose love in both the small and big moments. Let your story end with a very special, and personal, "And they lived happily ever after."

Day 316

Accept your partner for who they are—different than you!

You didn't marry your clone (thank goodness). Differences are part of the magic and the mess of marriage. You bring strengths they don't. They bring perspectives you never considered. And yes, sometimes you'll drive each other bananas. But acceptance means saying, "I love you, even when you make zero sense to me." Don't try to fix them. Learn from them. Celebrate the contrast. You don't have to agree on everything, but you *do* have to respect it. Because real love doesn't just tolerate differences, it invites them in and makes room at the table.

 Something to talk about: How has our relationship changed since we started dating?

Day 317

Your spouse is a gift, not a possession.

Love is not control. Your spouse isn't a project, a trophy, or a permanent fixture; they're a living, evolving human being who chooses to walk beside you each day. When you start treating them like a possession, you lose the beauty of mutual respect and freedom. Gratitude shifts everything. Wake up each day with the awareness that they're choosing *you*, and that choice deserves your kindness, trust, and humility. The healthiest relationships are rooted in freedom, not force. Honor your partner as the precious gift they are, not something you're entitled to keep.

Day 318

As you both grow and change, you each must learn to love that new version.

Marriage isn't about loving someone once, it's about loving them again and again as they evolve. Who your partner was five years ago might not be who they are today, and that's okay. Change is natural. Celebrate it. Get curious about who they're becoming. Ask questions. Stay connected. The version of your partner you fell in love with may have changed hairstyles, opinions, or priorities, but they're still the person who chose *you*. Choose them back. Growing together is a privilege, not a problem. Don't just hold on, keep reaching for each other.

 Conversation starter: What's a way we could use our unique skills to make a difference for others?

Day 319

Don't get caught up in routines.

Routines are helpful, but when life becomes all checklist and no connection, something's off. It's easy to let the day-to-day steal your spark. Shake it up. Sit in different chairs during dinner. Go on a mid-week date. Talk about something other than work and kids. Routines keep life moving, but rituals keep love meaningful. If you've stopped surprising each other, start again. If every night feels the same, create a reason to laugh. Keep some structure, sure, but make room for wonder. Your relationship deserves more than autopilot.

Day 320

Be each other's greatest cheerleader.

You already have plenty of critics in life. Your spouse shouldn't be one of them. Be the loudest voice applauding their wins and the softest one soothing their losses. Celebrate their ideas. Encourage their dreams. Be the person they look to when they need to believe in themselves again. You don't have to understand every passion, but you do need to support it. Marriage is about building something *together*, and that includes confidence. If they light up when they talk about it, let them know you see it. Cheer louder. Hug tighter. Brag boldly. Be their biggest fan and mean it.

 Ask each other: In what ways would you like us to continue evolving as partners?

Day 321

Be tolerant of your spouse's quirks.

You've got quirks. So do they. Some are cute, some are mildly maddening. But they're part of the package. Maybe it's how they load the dishwasher "wrong" or insist on sleeping with socks. Instead of trying to fix or shame them, find the funny. Find the familiar. These little quirks can become the fingerprints of your shared life, the details you'll miss most one day. Acceptance doesn't mean never getting annoyed; it means choosing love anyway. Let go of the need to correct everything. Sometimes the quirks are the spice in the soup.

Day 322

Marriage is held by thousands of tiny threads that hold you together through the years.

Small gestures are beautiful; they're the little things that truly bind you. Morning coffee. Inside jokes. Silent support. Texts that say, "I'm thinking of you." These threads, day after day, create a life. They're quiet but unbreakable. Over time, these moments weave a fabric that holds firm even when storms come. Don't wait for big milestones to show love. Weave it in everywhere. A marriage made of tiny threads has strength that steel can't match. Pay attention to the details because that's where your love story lives.

 Something to talk about: Is there a dream project or mission you've secretly always wanted to help with?

Day 323

Honor your partner by doing something out of the norm.

Respect isn't just about being polite; it's about being intentional. Go beyond the "thanks" and "pleases" of daily life. Write your partner a note. Toast them in front of friends. Brag about them at dinner. Show up to their big moment with bells on. When you show *honor*, you're saying, "I value who you are, publicly and privately." These gestures create a deep sense of being seen and celebrated. It doesn't have to be expensive or elaborate. Just unexpected, heartfelt, and genuine. Give them a reason to feel deeply appreciated today.

Day 324

Write out a renewal of your vows and place them in your home as a reminder of your love for each other.

Your wedding vows are more than poetic words; they're promises meant to last a lifetime. Writing them down and placing them in your home turns those sacred words into a daily visual cue. It's a reminder of the commitment, the hope, and the intention behind your love. On hard days, they'll ground you. On good days, they'll fill you with pride. Your vows don't belong in a memory; they belong in your everyday. Let them remind you of what you're building together, one choice and one loving act at a time.

 Conversation starter: If we had no fears, no limits — what kind of life would we build together from here?

Day 325

Choose to be your spouse's biggest fan and reject any thoughts of jealousy.

Your partner's success is *your* success. Their shine doesn't dim your light; it brightens the room you both share. If jealousy creeps in, check your mindset, not your marriage. Root for them with your whole heart. Celebrate without comparison. Cheer without competition. When your partner wins, you both move forward. Marriage isn't a race, it's a relay. Pass the encouragement baton often. Be the one who celebrates the loudest, listens the deepest, and lifts the highest. There's enough room for both of you to thrive, especially when you're cheering for the same team.

Day 326

Talk about retirement long before the time comes.

Retirement might sound like a never-ending vacation, but the reality includes identity shifts, new routines, and big adjustments. Talk about it *long before* the time comes. What do you each want retirement to look like? What's your rhythm going to be? Where do you settle down in the golden years? How much travel would you like? It's a significant chapter, and your marriage (and finances) needs a solid game plan. Honest, open conversations now can prevent resentment and confusion later. Get on the same page while you still have time to prepare. Plan towards a retirement you'll both love.

 Ask each other: What does retirement look like to you?

Day 327

Dance with your spouse around the living room.

You don't need a fancy night out to create romance. All you need is a little music, a little time, and a willingness to be delightfully silly. Dancing in the living room is about intimacy, playing, and being fully present. It's about pausing the world and turning your home into a love story. So, turn on your song, even if it's offbeat or awkward, and hold each other close. Let the dog watch. Let the kids giggle. Let love be light and unscripted. Some of the most memorable moments come from the unplanned ones, right in the middle of ordinary life.

Day 328

Do something out of the ordinary that proves your love is based on choice and nothing else.

Routine is comfortable, but love thrives on intention. Break out of your patterns occasionally and remind your partner that they are still worth the extra effort. Pack a surprise picnic. Book a spontaneous date. Leave a trail of sticky notes with reasons you love them. These actions say, "I'm still choosing you, not out of habit, but out of joy." Love by default becomes stale. Love by design? That keeps things alive. Don't wait for anniversaries or apologies to go above and beyond. Show up unexpectedly. That's when the magic happens.

 Something to talk about: What's one way we can bring more fun or playfulness into our relationship?

Day 329

Hold hands, even if you don't feel like it.

Physical touch can reconnect you when words fall short. Even if you're frustrated or distracted, reach out. That simple act says, "I'm still here. We're still a team." Holding hands can be grounding during conflict and magical in ordinary moments. It reminds you both that love is still in the room, even when your moods aren't in sync. Don't wait for a romantic mood—sometimes the tenderness follows the touch. Your hands are built for holding. So, use them often. You may be surprised how much connection can begin with your fingers.

Day 330

If your sex life gets boring, switch positions
(but NEVER partners!!)

Let's be real, routines sneak into every corner of marriage, including the bedroom. When intimacy starts feeling like a chore, don't panic, get playful. Switch things up, communicate more, and prioritize pleasure. Explore, laugh, reconnect. Don't treat it like a checklist, treat it like a dance. Just remember, if you're feeling unfulfilled, look *within* the relationship, not outside it. Boredom is not a betrayal; it's a cue to evolve together. Get curious about what lights each other up again. With a bit of creativity and a lot of trust, you can turn routine into rediscovery.

 Conversation starter: What's your favorite "memory" of an intimate moment we've shared?

Day 331

Identify one area of friction in your marriage and commit to making it better.

Every couple has *something*—budget battles, parenting philosophy clashes, silent tension over chores. Instead of pretending it doesn't exist, name it. Own it. Then, together, decide to work on it. Just one area. You don't have to fix everything overnight. Progress starts with awareness. Talk about it kindly. Make a plan. Revisit it. Improvement in one area often leads to healing in others. Think of it as spring cleaning for your relationship. Clear out the clutter of resentment and make space for fresh connection.

Day 332

Continue to grow and discover new interests to share.

Staying in love means continuing to discover each other. Don't just fall into the routine of surviving the week. Learn something new *together*. Take a cooking class, hike a new trail, start a book club for two. New experiences create new memories, and new memories keep things fresh. It's easy to let life get in the way, but shared interests are the glue that keeps couples close. You're not just co-parents, roommates, or co-workers in life. You're playmates, teammates, and partners in adventure. Stay curious. Stay connected. Keep growing.

 Ask each other: What's one little thing I could do to drive you wild, even on a regular Tuesday?

Day 333

Keep alone time with your spouse sacred.

With the demands of life—work, kids, errands—it's easy to lose the quiet intimacy that brought you together. Don't let that happen. Schedule time alone and guard it like it's priceless, because it is. Even 20 minutes on the couch, a walk after dinner, or breakfast before the chaos starts can work wonders. This isn't just "date night." It's heart time. It's reconnecting without distraction. No phones, no multitasking, just presence. Time alone is where the real conversations happen, the deeper love grows, and the flame keeps flickering. Make room for "just us."

Day 334

The thing that drew you to your partner will often be the thing that drives you crazy later on.

They were spontaneous. Adventurous. Free-spirited. And now? They're late to everything and can't stick to a plan. The truth is, our partner's most charming qualities often have a flip side, and once the honeymoon phase fades, those traits can test your patience. Instead of letting frustration fester, reframe it. That spontaneity still brings joy, just in different ways. The qualities that attract us are often the same ones that stretch us. Learn to love the whole person, not just the easy parts. Marriage isn't about changing them. It's about adjusting your lens with love.

 Conversation starter: What one volunteer project would you choose to do together this year?

Day 335

Never let the love you have for your spouse be displaced by kids.

Your love for your children is powerful, but it shouldn't replace your love for your partner. One strengthens the other. Giving your marriage attention makes your parenting stronger. Don't stop dating each other. Don't stop flirting. Don't stop being *two*, even while you're raising many. Your kids need to see what love looks like, so they know how to live it themselves. And one day, they'll grow up, and your spouse will still be there. Nourish that bond now. There's more than enough love to go around, just don't forget to give each other your share.

Day 336

Never make the one you love feel alone, especially when you're there.

Being physically present but emotionally absent is one of the loneliest experiences in marriage. You don't have to be glued at the hip, but when you *are* together, be *with* them. Look up. Engage. Ask how their day was. Show interest, even when you're tired. You don't need grand declarations, just consistent attention. Let them know: "I see you. I'm here with you." Emotional presence is more valuable than proximity. Don't leave your spouse feeling unseen in their own home.

 Ask each other: What new tradition could we start for just the two of us?

Day 337

*Never seek marriage advice from someone
who dislikes your spouse.*

Your marriage needs support, not sabotage. Be careful who you allow into your inner circle. If someone harbors resentment or bias against your partner, their advice may only add fuel to the fire. Choose wisdom over validation. Counsel should come from someone who cares about *both* of you, not just one side. Find people who want your relationship to thrive, whether it's a therapist, a trusted friend, or a mentor couple. Protect your marriage from anything or anyone that causes division.

Day 338

Never stop flirting with each other.

Flirting doesn't have an expiration date; it should grow right alongside your relationship. Send a cheeky text. Steal a kiss in the kitchen. Pinch their behind. Compliment their outfit. Laugh together like you used to. Flirting is the playful thread that reminds you both, "We're still us." You don't have to be young to keep the spark alive; you have to be intentional. Keep the twinkle in your eye and the mischief in your smile. When life feels heavy, flirting brings a sense of lightness. Don't stop wooing them, because being chosen over and over again never gets old.

 Conversation starter: What adventure (big or small) should we plan next?

Day 339

Never take each other for granted.

It's easy to assume your partner will always be there to pick up the slack, to laugh at your jokes, and to hold your hand through hard times, but love can grow weary if it's not acknowledged. Gratitude is fuel. Say, "Thank You" often for the little things, like taking out the trash or making coffee, and for the big things, like staying. Recognize the effort it takes to keep showing up. Nothing erodes closeness faster than being overlooked. So, notice. Appreciate. Speak it out loud. A little daily recognition goes a long way in keeping your connection vibrant.

Day 340

Give each other space to miss each other.

It might sound counterintuitive, but a little distance can bring you closer. When you spend every moment together, it's easy to slip into routine and take each other for granted. But when one of you pursues a hobby, spends time with friends, or simply enjoys a solo afternoon, you create room to recharge and rediscover yourself. That independence gives you fresh energy, stories to share, and even a spark of excitement when you come back together. Marriage isn't about constant proximity, it's about connection. And sometimes the best way to strengthen that connection is to give each other just enough space to say, "I missed you."

 Ask each other: When was a time you felt especially "seen" or understood by me?

Day 341

*Never threaten divorce to control
or manipulate your spouse.*

Throwing around the word "divorce" in moments of anger or fear is like tossing a grenade into your foundation. Even if you don't mean it, the damage lingers because threats erode safety. Love thrives in security, not in fear that one fight will send it all crumbling. If you're hurting, say so. If you're confused, say that. But don't weaponize something so sacred. Talk through issues without dangling ultimatums. Marriage isn't a game of power. It's a partnership that demands courage, vulnerability, and mutual respect, even in the messiest moments.

Day 342

Never trick your spouse into having children.

Parenting is one of the biggest journeys you'll ever take, and it demands unity from the start. Honesty isn't optional; it's vital. If one of you is unsure, unwilling, or simply not ready, it's not your job to push or manipulate. Tricking someone into parenthood can create long-term resentment and erode trust. The decision to have children must be made with shared conviction, mutual respect, and clear-eyed understanding of the road ahead. Marriage is about shared choices, not secret agendas. Respect your partner enough to wait until you're truly aligned to have hard conversations.

 Something to talk about: If our relationship was a movie, what would the title be right now?

Day 343

Never use sex as a weapon.

Never use sex as a weapon because intimacy should never be about control, punishment, or leverage. Withholding affection to make a point or force change doesn't solve problems; it creates distance and resentment. Sex isn't just physical, it's emotional, affirming, and one of the most powerful ways to stay connected as a couple. When it becomes a bargaining chip, the trust and safety that make intimacy meaningful begin to erode. If something's wrong in the relationship, talk about it openly instead of using the bedroom as a battlefield. Real love and intimacy thrive on honesty, vulnerability, and mutual care, not manipulation.

Day 344

No matter how comfortable you are with each other,
keep bathroom habits private.

Comfort is a beautiful thing, but a little mystery never hurts. You can be completely yourself without sharing *every* detail. Keeping a few personal boundaries can preserve attraction. It's not about shame; it's about maintaining a sense of romantic space. Just because you *can* talk through the door when you're on the toilet doesn't mean you *should*. Let some moments remain yours alone. The more you respect your privacy, the more you'll naturally protect theirs. Even soulmates can benefit from a bit of separation when it comes to the less glamorous side of daily life.

 Conversation starter: What's a silly or fun ritual we could start just for us?

Day 345

Plan and cook a meal together.

Cooking together is more than meal prep, it's a playful way to bond, communicate, and create something tangible. Pick a cuisine you've never tried. Shop for ingredients together. Put on music, laugh when things go sideways, and celebrate the finished dish, even if it's a mess. It's not about the food; it's about the memory. These shared experiences, especially the simple ones, deepen your connection. The kitchen can be a classroom, a dance floor, and a date night all rolled into one. Add a fun twist by selecting a different cuisine each month.

Day 346

Spend a moment to tell your spouse something that will make them feel special today.

Say something today that makes your spouse feel truly seen. Not just a generic "I love you," but something personal that reminds them why you chose them in the first place. Maybe it's how they light up a room, how they never give up, or how they make your coffee just right. Small words, big impact. A compliment, a thank-you, a little flirt—anything that lets them know they matter to you. Life moves fast, and we often assume they know how we feel. Don't assume. Speak love out loud. Your words might be the lift they didn't know they needed.

 Ask each other: If you went back to school right now, what would it be for?

Day 347

*Continue learning more about your spouse—
just don't be a pest about it.*

Even after years together, your spouse is still a book you haven't finished reading. Make it your mission to learn more about them, what they're thinking, dreaming, and struggling with. Ask questions. Be curious. But don't interrogate, because nobody likes a pop quiz over breakfast. The goal isn't control or obsession, it's connection. Let them know you're still invested, still fascinated, still eager to grow alongside them. When you keep learning about each other, you keep your love fresh. There's always something new to discover—just ask gently and listen with intention.

Day 348

Intentionally set aside quality time with your spouse.

There's always laundry. Always emails. Always another episode to binge-watch. But intentionally choosing to hit pause on something "important" so you can be present with your spouse sends a powerful message that says, "You matter more." Skip a solo trip to the gym and opt for a walk together. Let the dishes wait and postpone that phone call. Quality time isn't about quantity, it's about priority. Consistently choosing your partner over busyness builds trust and affection. Love doesn't demand constant attention, but it does ask to be chosen, especially in the small, seemingly insignificant moments.

 Conversation starter: What's one memory from our early years that still makes you smile?

Day 349

Give a lingering kiss for no reason at all.

There's something magical about a slow, unexpected kiss. Not the quick goodbye kind, but the kind that makes you pause. That says, "I still choose you." In the hustle of daily life, it's easy to forget how much touch matters. A lingering kiss doesn't need to lead to anything; it just needs to *mean* something. It's a moment of connection, a reset, and a reminder that you're more than just co-parents or roommates. Don't wait for a special occasion. Let love interrupt your day in the best way. Sometimes, one good kiss can say more than a dozen conversations.

Day 350

*Remove anything that is causing friction
in your relationship.*

You know what it is. That habit, distraction, person, or mindset that chips away at your connection. Maybe it's overworking, constant phone use, or a friendship that undermines your marriage. Whatever it is, be brave enough to name it, and strong enough to let it go. Relationships sometimes require pruning, not just watering. Cutting back the unhealthy makes room for growth. Your partner deserves your best, not what's left after everything else drains you. Protect your relationship like the sacred space it is. If something is pulling you apart, deal with it before it becomes the wedge you can't move.

 Ask each other: What's something new you'd like us to try together this year?

Day 351

Schedule a day for just the two of you.

You schedule dentist appointments, oil changes, and grocery runs, but when was the last time you put *your marriage* on the calendar? Time together doesn't just happen; it has to be carved out. Choose a day and protect it. No errands or chores. Just the two of you doing something that fills your cups. It could be something big, like a getaway, or small, like breakfast at your favorite diner. The point is connection. Time alone is where you remember who you are as a couple, not just as co-workers in the business of life. Prioritize it. Your love deserves a standing date.

Day 352

Share memories by looking at old photographs and talking about shared memories.

Pull out the photo albums or scroll through the photo folder on your phone. Remember the awkward haircuts, the road trips, the late-night laughs. Revisiting old memories does more than entertain, it strengthens your bond. It reminds you of where you've been, what you've overcome, and how far you've come together. Those shared experiences are the foundation of your story. Talking about them reignites joy, connection, and often, gratitude. It's easy to get stuck in the now, but the past holds some beautiful fuel for your future. Reminisce a little. Sometimes the best way forward is to look back—together.

 Conversation starter: What is our strongest bond?

Day 353

*If you don't show appreciation, your partner
may stop trying to please you.*

Gratitude is the love language that never goes out of style. If you want your partner to keep showing up, keep appreciating them not just on anniversaries or after grand gestures, but in the everyday moments. Say "thank you" when they take out the trash. Compliment them when they make dinner. Recognize the effort, even when it's routine. When someone feels seen, they keep giving. When they feel invisible, they retreat. Don't let busyness or comfort dull your expressions of appreciation. Keep it flowing. A well-timed "thank you" might be exactly what keeps love alive and growing.

Day 354

Love your spouse for who they are.

Marriage isn't always neat and tidy. Sometimes it's messy, unpredictable, loud, and hilarious. And that's okay. Loving someone fully means embracing their quirks, their big dreams, their offbeat humor, and even their chaos. You won't always understand them, but you can always choose to accept them. Don't spend your life trying to tone them down. Go for it with them. Jump into their wild ideas. Laugh at their jokes and dance when no one's watching, or even when they are! Love isn't about taming each other. It's about being safe enough to be fully seen and loved.

 Ask each other: What's one way we can create more laughter in our lives?

Day 355

Surprise each other every now and then.

Routine keeps life running, but surprise keeps love exciting. It doesn't have to be big. A handwritten note, a favorite snack, an unexpected compliment, or a spontaneous plan can all break up the ordinary in the best way. Surprises say, "I'm still thinking of you. You still matter to me." And they don't need a reason. That's the magic. When you surprise your partner, you add a little sparkle to the day, a gentle reminder that love is alive and worth paying attention to. So go ahead and be unpredictable in the sweetest way.

Day 356

Swap chores every now and then.

Want to understand your partner better? Step into their shoes—literally. If they usually do the laundry, offer to take over for a week. If they handle the bills, sit down and review them together. Swapping roles, even temporarily, builds empathy and respect. You'll gain a new appreciation for what they quietly do to keep your life running smoothly. It's not about perfection, it's about awareness. Bonus? It might even start some fun conversations or new routines. Marriage isn't about "mine" and "yours", it's about "ours." And every now and then, a little role-reversal can go a long way.

 Conversation starter: If we had a relationship motto, what should it be?

Day 357

Take a cooking class together.

It's not just about learning a new recipe; it's about understanding each other in a different context. A cooking class gets you out of your comfort zone, laughing at burnt sauces and celebrating small victories side by side. It's a playful way to communicate, cooperate, and reconnect. And hey, you get food at the end! Shared experiences like this create fresh memories and remind you that you're not just co-pilots in life, you're also teammates in fun. Whether you are culinary pros or can barely boil water, you'll leave with something special: a dish made with laughter and love.

Day 358

Identify an area of wrongdoing and ask for forgiveness.

It's not easy to admit when we've messed up, especially to the person we love most. But real strength in marriage comes from humility. Instead of brushing past mistakes or waiting for things to "blow over," pause and reflect. What did you say (or not say)? What did you do (or not do)? Then, without defensiveness or excuses, sincerely apologize. Ask for forgiveness not to clear your conscience, but to heal the bond. You're not just repairing a moment, you're reinforcing trust. A heartfelt apology says, "You matter more than my pride." And that kind of love is powerful.

 Finish this sentence: The items I hope to own are...

Day 359

Marriage is an evolution.

Every lasting relationship is full of endings: of versions of yourselves, of routines, and expectations. And that's not a bad thing. Growth requires letting go. You may end a season of selfishness, a pattern of miscommunication, or an old way of showing up that no longer fits who you're becoming. These endings pave the way for something better, more mature, loving, and genuine. Don't fear change in your relationship. Embrace it, grieve what needs to go, then celebrate what comes next. Love isn't static, it evolves. And with each ending comes a new beginning, a deeper knowing, and a stronger bond.

Day 360

Learn something new together.

Shared learning sparks connection. Whether it's salsa dancing, a new language, or trying to grow tomatoes on your balcony, the experience brings you into a space of curiosity *together*. It's playful, humbling, and often hilarious. You'll laugh, you'll mess up, and you'll cheer each other on. And the shared effort of figuring things out side by side builds memories that stick. It's not just about the skill; it's about the experience. Step into the unfamiliar, hand in hand. Learning something new as a couple reminds you that growth doesn't stop at "I do." It keeps going, and so do you.

 Conversation starter: If we could wake up anywhere tomorrow, where would you want it to be?

Day 361

Love withers away when growth stops.

A healthy marriage is always moving, learning, and evolving. You won't be the same people ten years from now, and that's a good thing! The key is to keep growing both as individuals and as a couple. Try new things together, encourage each other's dreams, and stay curious about who your partner is becoming. Stagnation breeds distance, but shared growth creates fresh energy and deeper connection. Love doesn't stay alive on its own, it thrives when you keep watering it with effort, curiosity, and the willingness to keep becoming better together.

Day 362

Love your partner when they least deserve it, because that's when they need it the most.

When your spouse is cranky, withdrawn, or pushing you away, that's not a cue to match the energy. That's your moment to lean in. Love isn't about rewarding good behavior; it's about showing up when it's *hard*. That's where trust deepens. Of course, love should have boundaries; it's not about accepting harm. But on the tough days, the grumpy days, the "I'm not myself" days, lead with grace. Remind them you're a safe place, even when they're unraveling. That kind of love heals. It doesn't mean tolerating everything, but it does mean choosing compassion when it matters most.

 Ask each other: What habit do you struggle with the most?

Day 363

Marriage is not all business.

Marriage can't run on grocery lists, calendar invites, and joint bank accounts alone. Yes, life brings responsibilities, but joy is what makes it all worth it. Laugh together. Plan silly dates. Dance in the kitchen or try something new that makes you both look ridiculous. Fun is the glue that keeps you close when stress tries to pull you apart. It reminds you of the friendship underneath the commitment. Don't wait for big vacations, build playfulness into your daily life. Because at the end of the day, love that laughs lasts.

Day 364

Marriage is the steady hand on the wheel when love hits a bump in the road.

There will be seasons where the spark dims, the rhythm shifts, and love feels more like a memory than a current mood. But marriage is the container that holds you through those seasons, giving you time and space to find your way back. It's not a failure, it's normal. Love ebbs and flows, but commitment provides a steady foundation while the feelings catch up. Be patient and kind. Stay curious about each other. The "fallback-in-love" moments are some of the sweetest, because they're built on choice, not infatuation. Keep showing up, because love will return, often stronger.

 Something to talk about: What makes you satisfied with your life?

Day 365

Staying in love doesn't just happen.

Staying in love is something you nurture, protect, and recommit to over time. It begins with chemistry, but it deepens with consistency. It's built in the small, often unnoticed moments: the way you speak to each other when you're tired, the grace you offer during a disagreement, the way you show up on ordinary Tuesdays. Real love isn't flashy, it's faithful. It's a quiet decision to stay soft in a hard world. To listen when it's easier to shut down. To hug when it would be simpler to walk away. A lasting marriage doesn't come from luck; it comes from effort, humility, and a shared willingness to grow together.

Protect what you've built. Keep choosing each other, especially when life gets busy, messy, or uncertain. Laugh often. Apologize freely. Don't stop flirting. Keep asking questions and learning who your partner is becoming.

Your "happily ever after" isn't a final destination, it's a living, breathing story you write together. And the more intention you bring to it, the more beautiful it becomes. This is love, not a chapter you close, but the story you keep writing.

 Ask each other: What younger couples could we mentor to help them have the best relationship possible?

What's Next?

Congratulations on completing this book filled with wisdom from couples eager to share their experiences! As you've journeyed through the pages, you've discovered the profound truth expressed in the quote:

"Wisdom is the reward of experience and should be shared."

Let the lessons shared in this book inspire you and your partner to move forward with purpose. Your personal experiences and lessons are your unique wisdom, which are valuable treasures meant to be shared. Each of us has the power to uplift and inspire others. Let's keep learning from each other, growing together, and spreading positivity and wisdom wherever life takes us.

About the Author

Jen Fort is a writer, coach, encourager, and lifelong connector who believes lasting love is built on wisdom, laughter, and daily choices. As the creator of the *Wisdom & Warnings* series, she gathers life lessons from real people and shares them with honesty, humor, and heart. *Happily Ever After* was born from her desire to give engaged and married couples practical, playful wisdom to help love thrive. Through her writing, Jen reminds couples that marriage isn't about perfection—it's about building something real, beautiful, and meant to last.

Visit www.iamjenfort.com to:

- Pay it forward by sharing your favorite nuggets of wisdom and perhaps have yours included in future books.
- Receive free resource suggestions.
- Be the first to know about upcoming Wisdom & Warnings book releases.
- Find out how you can further benefit from Jen's life mission to encourage and share life lessons!